## Dudley Crawford

# Stumbling Over Stardust

*I have spent my life watching,*
*not to see beyond the world,*
*merely to see, great mystery,*
*what is plainly before our eyes.*
*I think the concept of transcendence*
*is based upon a misreading of the creation.*
*With all respect to heaven,*
*the scene of the miracle is here,*
*among us.*

Marilynne Robinson

*To treat life as less than a miracle*
*Is to give up on it.*

Wendell Berry

Author as young astronomer,
circa 1958

Print ISBN: 978-1-66783-033-9
eBook ISBN: 978-1-66783-034-6

# Preface

Blogs became fashionable over the past couple of decades, and this writer became a blogger in his later life. The first edition, published in early March of 2019, was entitled *Heaven on Earth* and presented a picture of me in my backyard homemade observatory in the 1950's peering into the dark night. My hobbies of astronomy and photography would eventually merge with my pursuit of theology and my vocation of ministry. Upon retirement in 2005, I realized that I had developed the skills necessary for wordsmithing which would render me capable of synthesizing my thoughts into new and emerging field of blogging.

The span of history for these chapters includes the tumultuous years of the Trump presidency and the worldwide COVID-19 pandemic. Some of these essays are therefore political in nature while others may seem like a sermonette. The object of each is to make a point that just might be important for us, and to make it quickly.

# Grateful Remembrances

My heartfelt appreciation to all those who contributed to this work. To Mamaw, who was my kindergarten teacher and the one who led me to be a reader of some wonderful books at a young and impressionable age. Those public-school teachers of ages past who gave me the alphabet and the words and some of the courage necessary to build a new world with those old tools. Those fellow students who shared the journey. Those college and seminary professors who led me way outside the box and way out of any provincial thinking. To my family who endured my many yarns and who gave me stories beyond my imagination and the colorful tapestry of many emotions and wonderful memories.

To my working colleague and son-in-law Gregg Cagno, who provided the technical expertise and guided me through the valley of the shadow of the World Wide Web into your hands and before your eyes right now. From the original conception to the release of each Sunday morning chronicle, he was the Wizard of Oz behind our screens.

Dudley Crawford<br>
West End, NC – February 2022

# A Quick Biography

 For the last sixteen years or so, Dudley Crawford has been pretending to be a retired minister of the Presbyterian Church USA. Some of the people of the West End Presbyterian Church thought he had retired long before that, but he just looked dead tired because he had served that congregation for 22 years, bringing it from a little church in the wildwood with less than a hundred members to a wild church in those same woods of nearly 600 congregants and active participants hailing from all over the map geographically, theologically and politically.

Born of natural causes in Canton, Mississippi nearly 80 years ago, he grew up a hardcore catechism kid in the reformed tradition. He has a BA degree from Millsaps College in Jackson, MS. and a degree from Union Presbyterian Seminary in Richmond. After serving two churches in Mississippi from 1968 to 1975, he became Director of Admissions at St. Andrews Presbyterian College in Laurinburg. He moved to West End in 1983. In the late 1970's he also served as an adjunct professor of preaching in the Doctor of Ministry program at Columbia Theological Seminary.

He and his wife, Peggy, have lived in Seven Lakes for nearly four decades. They have 4 children and 5 grandkids who affectionately refer to Dudley as "Big Daddy", a name to which he has aspired most of his life so far.

Read more at *StumblingOverStardust.com*.

# Contents

# Heaven on Earth

Growing up, I was captivated by the stars above our backyard smack dab in the middle of Mississippi. When darkness settled on the face of the earth, I was out there aiming my little telescope toward the heavens. With only a small window of sky between the pecan and magnolia trees, I was able to see enough to start dreaming about becoming an astronomer.

When I was fifteen, the Soviet Union launched Sputnik, and the space race was on in earnest. You could see that scudder through my homemade observatory, and neighbors would wander into my backyard for a glimpse. I upgraded this hobby by grinding the mirror and constructing a bigger telescope for peering even deeper into that wide open space above us. I entered college to major in physics and astronomy and graduated a religion major headed for seminary.

When you move from peering into space to prayerful reading of religious texts, you develop a crick in your neck and confusion in your heart and mind and soul. This switch was also a realignment of concerns and concepts. For example, I remember thinking as a kid that the church seemed to have all the truth on its side to convince you that creation took place in six or seven days nearly five thousand years ago. Then science used geological and astronomical facts to show that it was created over eons.

While appreciating the factual features of astronomy and the other sciences, I came to understand that many of the truths of the faith were not quite what they seemed. I discovered more mystery surrounding God than the verifiable truth. So, I turned my gaze from the heavens to the earth where I began to see all sorts of mysterious miracles that opened up a whole universe within me.

Over my rather quick three quarters of a century of circling the sun, I have found many centers of warmth which are smaller than a mole hill under my feet and larger than any mountain I've ever seen. Realizing that all of us are children of the universe, composed of carbon that started back at the Big Bang, that's enough to warm the cockles of your heart 'til kingdom come on earth as it is in heaven. Or maybe we can't see what's been here forever.

3/10/2019

# Planetary Patriotism

"Dear God, I am an American. What are you?" That's what one small child wrote in her letter to God. Another asked, "Who draws the lines around the countries?" Those are fairly simple questions, but they cut to the complexities of a world order that is still being driven by some old nationalisms. Mark Twain once noted that "Man is the only patriot. Sets himself within the lines of his own country and hires assassins at a great price to protect those lines. We have done this so that there is not an acre of earth left that is in the rightful possession of its owner."

While the originals of the species might have lacked for creature comforts at the dawn of civilization, they must have enjoyed the peace and quiet. No one had bothered to create an enemy. Between their flat-earth existence and our society that looks back on the planet earth from a space shuttle, something went haywire. Someone started drawing those lines around the countries, and countries started fighting for more than their fair share of turf. Territories were staked out, countries emerged, governments were established, and weapons were invented to protect us from — of all things — each other. We have met the enemy, and they are us.

The new world order is built upon the precarious foundations of old world concepts where a little competition never hurt anyone and a little war every now and then was a necessary evil to prove that some of us at least could be kings of the hills by virtue of who might happen to have the bigger bomb this year. That old order seems to be fading fast these days, and the futility of war grows more apparent. If we learned anything from all the intervening wars since, we have understood once again that wars still cause more problems than they solve. They aren't worth the hassle in a world where countries are becoming more interdependent and the ecological resources more precious to all the earth's inhabitants.

Like Columbus, the world is beginning to wonder if there might be a new way of life beyond the bleak horizons of our limited liabilities of national patriotisms. Like Neil Armstrong, we all need to start taking a bunch of steps for Man and Woman and All our Children that will lead us to become passionate patriots of this spaceship Earth whose allegiance to the common welfare of this global neighborhood is more important than who wins the next war. Maybe God is wondering when we will finally draw the line and become responsible citizens of that world-wide Kingdom without boundaries.

3/17/2019

# Democracy of the Dawn

All creatures, great and small, enjoy the democracy of dawn. Like the biblical rains, the sun shines on the just and the unjust. Each day arrives as a gift to be enjoyed. Each day begins as a clean slate ready for each artist to create a little piece of their own destiny. Each day is a portion of a patchwork quilt that will make up all the days of our lives. And no matter our condition or station in life, the day ahead is ours for the taking. *Carpe diem*, and all that jazz.

The poet's prayer speaks something for us all: "Brave Helios, wake up thy steeds; bring the warmth the countryside needs." The pre-dawn darkness gives way to the steel grey which yields to that faint orange glow of morning's quiet entry. Once again, the spotlight begins to shine upon this stage of a world, and the actors move from comforts of slumber into their positions for the dramatic episodes that will include comedy and tragedy all their live-long days.

The early morning brings out the best in most people. Others live by the code emblazoned on a t-shirt: "I don't do mornings!" But for those who do mornings, there's a peculiar glory about the earth and a new lease on life itself. We wake up and smell the coffee and kiss spouse and kids. We look in the mirror and hardly notice that we're another day older. We're alive, and the morning glory is beginning to bloom in us.

While some might find it difficult to sing "Oh what a beautiful morning…", many believe that each day can be a roll of the dice. Others feel that this is a brand-new chance to join whatever forces are at work in this world to create Eden all over again in order to recall the original blessing. By the end of day, we once again look forward to the awaiting slumber that is our preparation for the dawning of the next chapter in the days of our lives.

In Judaism, the day begins at dusk and nightfall. Our days begin with rest for the coming morning. It's a great idea. When I hit the sack, I am "dead to the world". My slumber renews my soul and refreshes my body. Like resetting the memory in my computer. But when morning gilds my skies, I am recreated and ready for a brand-new day as fresh as the morning dew. It's almost a resurrection of the body. Almost Easter every morning for the rest of our livelong days.

3/24/2019

# Homegrown

They are not the first thing to open in spring; they are late bloomers. By mid-April, when the dogwood sheds its blossoms to create a white mantle around its trunk, sign painters are freshening the plywood placards that bear the welcomed words: "HOMEGROWN TOMATOES" or "FRESH STRAWBERRIES — PICK YOUR OWN". Out of their winter's hibernation, the produce stands emerge once again. Undaunted by the dormant months, they spread the good news that the earth is once again about to create its glorious garden of homegrown goods. Mother Nature is open for business.

Many of us have our favorite spots, and we'll go miles out of the way to stop on the side of the road to select Vidalia onions, green peppers and corn still dressed in its natural shuck and tasseled with silk threads. We speak to the vendors in down home ways as we ask their opinion on this cantaloupe or that squash. We want to know on whose land they were produced.

What is it about "homegrown" that works its marketing magic on us? As much as it is the charm of choosing fresh vegetables as close to the farm as possible, it is also a subtle prompter of the sweet memories of our childhood when the backyards of our earlier springs were full of seeds carefully chosen and planted with hope, the soil lovingly watered and the rabbits carefully kept at bay until the fruits of our labors finally appeared.

My Granddaddy seemed to be the wisest gardener among us, though I never did see his green thumb that everyone said he had. Not only did he know when and how to plant the stuff, he knew exactly when it was ripe and ready to pick. I also believe he knew why we gardened, but he never let us in on the secret. We simply filled our baskets and bags with the harvest. We sat at the table, gave thanks, and spent the whole meal in utter amazement that our very own okra was the best in the whole wide world!

Like the plants in those gardens, all of us are also homegrown varieties of human beings. Whether we grew up in the ideal soil of a happy homes or the almost barren dirt of homes barely held together against the ravages of hard times, we know in our bones that that's where our roots were put into the earth. In a sense, the garden is our common ground. And it is holy ground as well. Whether it was in the lost paradise of Eden or the backyard oasis of our childhood, all of us are homegrown. And the simple taste of a fresh tomato sandwich becomes soul food for us all and as nourishing as mother's milk.

Joni Mitchell's haunting song hits home: "We are stardust, we are golden/ We are billion year old carbon, / And we've got to get ourselves back to the garden."

3/31/2019

# A Little Church in the Wildwood

*There's a church in the valley in the wildwood*
*No lovelier place in the dell*
*No spot is so dear to my childhood*
*As the little brown church in the dell.*

Most old-timers will recall with great fondness these words of an old gospel song. There was such a church that was dear to my childhood in the middle of Mississippi called the Chapel of the Cross. Built by slaves in the 1850's, it was part of Annandale Plantation, just across the road from my people's home place. It's Gothic Revival architecture drew heavily from 14th-century English country churches. It had a proud heritage within the Episcopal branch of the Church and had a unique history dating back to the early days of the state before the war of northern aggression.

My mother's people were buried in the backyard of this little brown church, and in the spring and summer the Bennett clan who were still on top of this native soil would all gather for the task of cleaning the grounds of the family burial plots. The men did most of the clearing while the women prepared the picnic and watched us kids. Once they started telling those stories while sitting around the picnic tables, the young cousins would get lost in the old, abandoned sanctuary where we would "play church".

For whatever reasons, the Chapel had been abandoned as a viable worship center and had even been vandalized during the

1940's and 50's. That's when the young Bennett cousins would turn it into a sanctuary fit for the God's chosen youth group. Brother Jimmy would play the old pump organ while cousin Fanny Wee would beguile us all with ghost stories. Rocks from the driveway would be brought in as offerings and tastefully strewn on the empty altar. Nonsense was used in lieu of incense!

In my travels around the world since those ancient of days, I've wandered into many historic cathedrals that would hold a dozen of those quaint little Chapels at once. Ornate grandeur crowned them as sacred sanctuaries to the glory of God or God's competition. Many of them took generations to complete. But none seemed to hold a candle to that sweet little church in those Mississippi woods.

We were innocent yet amazing liturgical celebrants creating a wild kind of church in our meager imaginations. We were not only kith and kin, but we were also the children of God without knowing it, like staring stardust in the face. Later, we would realize that we were also sisters and brothers of the slaves who fabricated those bricks and walls to create a church for the people who thought they owned them.

Reckoning with that historical fact, we could feel so many shoulders – black and white – on which we were standing on that holy ground. This little church in the wildwood and the holy memories from my own childhood within her slave-made walls would launch my religious phantoms and fantasies suitable for years to come and ground me in the sweet harmony and mystery of all my people who were all God's precious children. God's holy family.

4/7/2019

# Whistling Dixie

On a recent journey through eastern North Carolina, I spied this rather large Confederate flag planted in front of a tomb in a cemetery beside a country church. The stars and bars were gently flowing in the summer breeze, creating the only movement under the large oaks covering the burial places and recreating a momentary motion that we once thought was gone with the wind.

I wondered out loud: When did Dixie die? Else what is she doing in this graveyard among the dead? Did someone finally do her wrong and do her in? There's a song somewhere about the day that Dixie died, and this must have been where it happened.

Of course, having grown up in Dixie, I know how most of the myth goes. We are all supposed to save our Confederate money, boys, 'cause the South will rise again! Old times there are not forgotten. I remember when they played "Dixie" before certain events in the Magnolia state, you would stand and place your right hand over your heart. We only observed Confederate Memorial Day in my hometown and not the other one. And anybody north of Memphis was either a communist, a Yankee or an outside agitator. "Forget, Hell! " was the favorite bumper sticker for Chevy pickups with shotguns in their rear windows. Some southern folks were a little more tolerant. They allowed how if those people who started the war of northern aggression would only give us back the silver, we'd forget the whole thing.

Several years ago, Mitch Landrieu, the Mayor of New Orleans, delivered a speech on the removal Confederate monuments in the Big Easy. Listen to a few of his poignant words: *This is, however, about showing the whole world that we as a city, that we as a people are able to acknowledge, to understand, to reconcile, and more importantly, choose a better future for ourselves, making straight what has been crooked and making right what was wrong. Otherwise, we will continue to pay a price with discord, with division, and yeah, violence.*

*History cannot be changed. It cannot be moved like a statue. What is done is done. The Civil War is over. The Confederacy lost — and we're better for it. Surely, we are far enough removed from this dark time to acknowledge that the cause of the Confederacy was wrong. And in the second decade of the 21st century, asking African Americans — or anyone else for that matter — to drive by property that they own; occupied by reverential of men who fought to destroy the country and deny that person's humanity seems perverse. It seems absurd. Century-old wounds are still raw because, you see, they never healed right in the first place. So here is the essential truth: We are better together than we are apart. Indivisibility is our essence.*

Lest we forget, the blood of Gettysburg and Vicksburg was spilled on those fields by Rebels and Yanks who had a cause for which they gave the last full measure of devotion. And the new nation has risen out of the graves of slaves and slave owners. And there's really no point to whistling Dixie as the antithesis of today's reality. We are overcoming much of the tragedy – the bitterness and bigotry and racism of our past and someday, by the grace of Almighty God, we shall all overcome.

4/14/2019

# Peculiar Gardeners

Gardeners are a peculiar lot who, like their gardens, come in all sorts of shapes and sizes. First-rate gardeners produce bushels of veggies each year; others put a tomato plant in the flower bed and call it a garden. During the heart of winter, the full-bloodied gardener is already imagining the produce, while turning the good earth in preparation for that day when the seed can be planted. There is a time to sow, and the true gardener can't wait for that day to dawn.

What is it that attracts some people to this horticultural endeavor? Is it some primitive drive for survival? Or, on a more noble plane, maybe there is a vocational link with our first parents' occupation as one of those clowns in Shakespeare's "Hamlet" describes it in an attempt to plan the burial of Ophelia: "There is no ancient gentlemen but gardeners, ditchers, and grave makers. They hold up Adam's profession." When our fore parents are driven from the automatic Garden of Eden, they started tilling the earth to grow their own grub. And it looks like their descendants will till it 'til kingdom come.

Ever since leaving the Garden of Eden, we've been trying to harvest the earth. Part of it is for the survival of the species. Without the potatoes and bread and okra and kale, we could not live. Yet, we do not live by bread alone, and there's a transcendent quality about gardening that is the soul's delight. It is communing with Mother Nature, but more than that. There is a tie that binds gardeners into a fellowship. When you till the earth, you begin to understand the common ground, double entendre intended.

One of the funniest stories in all of the scriptures is when Mary first arrived at the tomb on what would become the first Easter. She had no earthly idea of what was going on and innocently mistook Jesus for the cemetery gardener. That might be a fairly good supposition. One of his simplest descriptions of kingdom life was "…like a grain of mustard seed, which, when sown upon the ground, is the smallest of all the seeds on earth; yet when it is sown it grows up and becomes the greatest of all shrubs, and puts forth large branches, so that the birds of the air can make nests in its shade." He used wheat and tares and lilies of the field and barren fig trees to make his gospel points. Not sure he would be cover material for Garden and Gun magazine, but he spoke with some authority about this great garden in which all God's children are invited to the table together.

"Are you a gardener?" asked the Easter morning Mary. You bet your life he was a gardener… a master gardener, double entendre still intended. Those early birds in the graveyard that morning almost stumbled over that stardust right in front of them. And the angels that morning asked us all a hard question: why are you seeking the living among the dead?

4/21/2019

# Applying Ourselves

Public school report cards were a kind of nemesis for some of us. They were tell-tell evidence of our achievement — or lack thereof — and your parents had to sign them to confirm their having seen same.

The grade portion was quite to the point of how you made the grade utilizing the A to F scale. On the back was a small amount of space for each six-week grading period for the teacher to make her or his comments. I frequently received the familiar notice that I needed to "apply myself more". While the message might have been code between teacher and parents, no one ever explained quite fully how in heaven's name I had anything more to apply to myself.

After the first or second reading of the report card, my Mother, bless her heart, would emphasize how I really needed to "apply myself with the added proviso: "If you are ever going to amount to something, then you had better…". Depending on the topic, the next line had something to do with practicing the piano, or doing your homework, or keeping your room immaculate, or getting off the phone. I'm seventy-seven and still wondering how to apply myself if I ever want to amount to anything!

But there is an antidote to this dreadful dilemma so dramatically expressed by Josephine, my grandmother's helper: "Lord, have mercy! Now ain't you something!" In that affirmative credo she meant that we were conceived and brought forth and given life. The Creator concocts the wonderful chemistry of this universe and endows you with so much that you are indeed better off right at the very beginning. And then, to beat all, the grace! The amazing grace. The splendid and marvelous grace that states before the creation and all these witnesses that you are created by God and called to be a child of God.

Now, ain't you already something special! This is as good as it gets! Without all the striving and pushing and competing and toiling and spinning, there's already something about you that's as beautiful as the lily of the field. And there's a carefree spirit within you that's as free as the birds of the air or the sheep in the twenty-third pasture.

Once I realized how much grace applied to my life and heard the rumor that God just might grade us on a curve, I was free from the fear of failure. While the law of averages was on my side, t'was grace lifted me from the quagmire of under-achievement and made me something special. That's as good as it gets.

4/28/2019

# Discovering What's Here

Revisionist historians have made their point: Columbus did not "discover" America in 1492. You can't discover what has already been there for centuries even though it might be twenty thousand leagues under the sea.

When boat builders figured out that sailing crafts could go a long way, and cartographers figured out that there were no dragons on the earth's edge, Christopher convinced Isabel that he could head west in order to go east. When his armada of three vessels pulled up on foreign shores of a new world, the native people on the beach discovered Europeans for the first time.

Perhaps the most significant example of this subject was another Italian by the name of Galileo Galilei. To understand the remarkable nature of this discovery, you need to remember that everybody believed the earth was flat. Or some folk held that it was geocentric with stars and planets circling the earth like that Greek Ptolemy said it was. In 1543, a Polish fellow, Copernicus, asserted it might be heliocentric with the sun as the center. Fifty years later, while peering at Jupiter's four moons through a telescope, Galileo discovered that Copernicus had hit the right nail on the right head.

Isaac Newton was barking up the same tree when he figured out the laws of gravity by observing objects falling. Nothing unusual about falling objects, but what in tarnation brings them down to earth in the seemingly same manner.

It's just a matter of paying attention. A researcher in London returned from his vacation in Scotland to discover that the petri dishes in his lab were covered with a strange kind of fungus-looking material. Rather than just clean up this apparent mess, Alexander Fleming unearthed the miracle drug we know as penicillin. Paying attention paid off!

Our son was working in the labs of Eastman Chemical Company trying to figure out a different kind of plastic. When he was rambling through some old files of experiments that were deemed worthless, he became intrigued. When he reconsidered the notion, it led him to rediscover some secret ingredients for what would become Tritan, the company's next generation of co-polymer and its economic boom in the industry.

And don't forget the printing press. Gutenberg figured out the puzzle of movable letters and numbers. He happened to be that "type" of fellow who could see the obvious in what everyone thought was oblivious. Have you been paying attention to the words you are reading? It's all in a font known as Georgia. Right between your eyes and under your nose. Eureka!

5/5/2019

# She Bothered

Does it ever bother you that some of our words can take on different meanings under different circumstances? Take the words like "bother" and "trouble". Within a simple change of nuance, their meanings can be suddenly opposite.

At a dinner party recently one of the guests looked at the center piece of fresh flowers and exclaimed: "You bothered!" She was expressing her delight in how the host had bothered so much to take care of so many details in such an elegant manner. Which translated into an extraordinary compliment and a splendid expression of gratitude that someone would go to such trouble for the likes of us enjoying the meal.

"Getting into trouble" and "going to a lot of trouble" are two sides of the same word, but they are kissing cousins to "bother". "Don't call me…I don't want to be bothered" is the polar opposite to "I'm honored that you bothered enough to call."

So just maybe we would all do well in bothering to do better in how we show our appreciations and affections. First of all, it's figuring out the indicators. We can be so self-centered or self-absorbed that we just don't get it when someone has gone out of their way to do something beyond the norm of nice. We need a special intuitive knack and a sensitive interpersonal radar that may be nullified by lack of use over time.

When you realize that your host has gone out of her way to make the evening soiree very special because she deeply cares about those people at the table, the proper response goes much deeper than table manners or southern etiquette. Even chivalry can't hold a candle to such an authentic gesture. A "thank you" simply said from the heart and head is good for a start until it finally dawns on you that there are no adequate words.

There's a group of people who spring to mind when I think of all the bother they went through on our behalf: our mothers! They nurtured us in their wombs; gave us birth at a certain painful cost; cleaned our diapers; put up with our adolescence; and loved us without flinching. Because they bothered to love us like that, we should be grateful beyond words. Our silence can become gratitude. Rumi reminds us: *There's a voice that doesn't use words. Listen.*

5/12/2019

# Here's Looking at You, Our Lady

On the surface of things, she appeared to be her old self. An ancient of days who once sat crowned in glory. Where, for over eight centuries, generations of knees had bent in prayers of supplication. Rosaries said, and the relic Crown of Thorns treasured and venerated. But just around the corner of her timeless face, you could see the outlines of the tragic consequences of a consuming Holy Week fire.

For the sake of safety, approaches to the sacred ground surrounding Notre Dame were blocked by metal fences and armed guards, while she sat there beyond reproach of any sort. Her dignity and honor still in tact while machines craned their repairing cargo all around her.

In her surrounding channels of the River Seine, boats loaded with tourists from every nation under the sun skim the surface of her long legacy as if it were merely an ancient dream of some historic past. They come and go as if seeking Michelangelo or some legions of the French dreams until the currents take them toward Eiffel's tower, still timeless and standing erect against a setting sun.

The grand Lady of Paris, though brought down to earth by calamity and gravity, seems more like a Phoenix than a collapsed Cathedral. Waiting for that holy spirit to restore her windows of glory and open her doors to all people. Deflated but not undone, the quiet mother of all cathedrals remembers the flames and combustion. Like that old Greek bird, in her ancient ashes, a new holy place will emerge, and her flying buttresses will bring life once again to all her dear people and tourist alike. Her mighty bells will toll over the Parisian skies with songs of melodious praise. Choirs echoing *Ave Marias* or Gregorian chants ricocheting under vaulted roof. Dancing flames of candles lighting dark space in loving memories of the quick and the dead. From requiem to rejoicing. From ruin to restoration.

From charred relic to rekindled glory. All of us say a little prayer for that high and holy hope.

We might always have Paris but let us never take for granted those holy places throughout our lives that are susceptible to tragedy. While she seems like a hunchback invalid at the moment, Notre Dame continues to teach all of us about the sacred right in the middle of the secular.

*Writer's note: I am in France for most of May and spent a few days in Paris which inspired this blog.*

5/19/2019

# Politically Correct

Politics and religion tend to be the great dividers in our culture and country these days. Our *e pluribus unum* seems to be out of wack, and "under God" has more meanings than one can imagine. Part of the issue is semantics. Take the phrase "politically correct". Of course, the term itself seems like an oxymoron in an era in which the political machinery is driven by negative motives that pollute the air with cynicism. The term is inaccurate for the purpose that it engenders. Let me explain.

To be politically correct in one's parlance, you must be sensitive to all the differences within the society. All those isms: racism, ageism, sexism, and all the others that delineate groups within the culture who are seeking reform through language sensitivity. In the introduction to his best seller, Politically Correct Bedtime Stories, James Finn Garner illustrates what I mean in this apologetic sentence: "If, through omission or commission, I have inadvertently displayed any sexist, racist, culturalist, nationalist, regionalist, ageist, lookist, ableist, sizeist, speciesist, intellectualist, socioeconomicist, ethnocentrist, phallocentrist, heteropatriarchalist, or any other type of bias as yet unnamed, I apologize..."

The irony is that reform itself is never politically correct. It's the opposite. Examples run the calendar of human achievements. Galileo was politically incorrect for suggesting that the earth may not be the center of the universe. Martin Luther was politically off the mark when he suggested that each human being could read and interpret the scriptures for himself or herself. Uppity women rather than the mild-mannered ones finally got the right for women to vote. Martin Luther King was morally right for suggesting that we ought to have a country where people are judged by the content of their character rather than the color of their skin. Unfortunately, in most political circles, the racial difference mattered greatly. And still does.

Jesus himself was finally crucified for being politically incorrect. Throughout his life, he was always doing things that went against the grain of conventional wisdom within his own religion. He spoke to a Samaritan woman at the well. He ate with prostitutes, tax collectors and other scoundrels. He cleaned house at the local temple of the money changers. Neither Judaism nor Rome could handle his political ineptness. So they conspired to rid the scene of such a trouble maker. Even in today's political arena, Jesus would have a hard time selling his idea of the great judgment in Matthew 25, when he declares that the nations will be held accountable for their caring for the hungry, the stranger, the sick and the prisoner. Dream on. It would take an act of Congress for that to happen!

5/26/2019

# esse quam videri

To look at her one would jump to the conclusion that all was well in her world. That she had her act together. That she was a smooth operator. A person for all seasons. But beneath the outward appearance, and not necessarily deep down but just below the surface there was this frenzy of insecurity and this fear of failure. She knew how to look like humanity personified, but the constant struggle she faced was to half-way meet the projected image on the screen of her existence. To do that meant to be on guard, constantly striving to be more than she was.

Whoever she was, she is someone with whom we can all identify. For her struggle is what all of us do in different degrees. There are times when living seems like one big game of pretend, which was fun when we were children, but a bit absurd for adults.

Teenagers know this feeling better than any of us. Frederick Buechner, in <u>Whistling in the Dark</u>, describes this aptly in a portrait of an adolescent standing in front of a mirror: "The opaque glance and the pimples. The fancy new nakedness they're all dressed up in with no place to go. The eyes full of secrets they have a strong hunch everybody is on to. The shadowed brow. Being not quite a child and not quite a grown-up either is hard work, and they look it. Living in two worlds at once is no picnic. One of the worlds, of course, is innocence, self-forgetfulness, openness, playing for fun. The other is experience, self-consciousness, guardedness, playing for keeps. Some of us go on straddling them both for years."

It is hard work, keeping our fingers crossed all our lives. Only pretending to live. Playing house. Playing work. Playing recreation. Playing church. In order to seem like living, both to others and to ourselves. We learn somewhere along the way to promote ourselves to be more than we can be. Projecting ourselves — our better selves. The selves we wish we could be. Until there is a blurred distinction between reality and the projection. Just like The Great Pretender that the Platters crooned about in the 50's...*too real is this feeling of make believe/ too real when I feel what my heart can't conceal.*

Even in church, we have learned to define the Christian life in certain ways; recognize that we are not quite in the ballpark; but pretend that we are close enough. The late Baptist minister, Carlyle Marney, used to say: "People go to church not to be who they are, but to be who they hope to God they look like they are." The Lord of life invites us all to live just as we are. We don't have to be great pretenders. No need to put on airs.

Or as the motto of North Carolina puts it: *esse quam videri* –"to **be** rather than to seem."

6/2/2019

# Looking Glass

In Lewis Carol's sequel to Alice in Wonderland, the Walrus speaks quite eloquently to the Carpenter: *"The time has come,"* the *Walrus said, "To talk of many things: of shoes – and ships – and sealing wax – of cabbages – and kings – and why the sea is boiling hot – and whether pigs have wings."*

Though not the most profound paragraph in English lit, this little vignette has always been a favorite. In that topsy-turvy world on the other side of that looking glass things appear to be wicky-wacky if not catawampus. Like stumbling over stardust, you never seem to know where you will land.

A similar expression that's somewhat in vogue these days is seeing things through "different lenses". When we have some sort of epiphany or revelation, we might look at someone or something in a "whole new light". Or if you are cockeyed optimist, you might be accused of seeing the world through rose-colored glasses; those folks can make a spectacle out of themselves.

The kaleidoscope is a fascinating optical instrument providing a variety of symmetrical and colorful patterns in the eye of the beholder. By rotating it, the particles and mirrors do their magic. A magnifying glass helps us see the magnificence of a butterfly wing. I remember my first microscope and watching the paramecium from the pond squiggling on that glass slide. Then came the telescope that brought the bigger world closer and the craters of the moon right into my backyard.

No wonder Galileo tops my charts as the best heretic of all times. You know the story...the moons of Jupiter led him to ultimately surmise that the earth was not the center of anything in particular. The Church of the Almighty Answers, of course could not abide such a thing. During Galileo's trial, Cardinal Bellarmine put it like this: "To assert that the earth revolves around the sun is as erroneous as to claim that Jesus was not borne of a virgin." Galileo remained under house arrest until his death, and only recently has the Church indicated that they may have been wrong about him.

If the truth be known, looking through any optical device may be hazardous to your understanding of the universe. The Hungarian novelist, Zsolt de Harsanyi, captures the essence of such a dilemma in this moving scene from his novel, The Star Gazer: *"Listen, Galileo! The science of the world was built on the pillars of Aristotelian wisdom. For two thousand years men have lived and died in the belief that the earth is the center of the universe and man the lord of it… After Aristotle, Our Lord Jesus Christ descended upon earth and saved us, giving us His wonderful gift, Christianity. This Christianity has perfected Aristotle, spiritualized him, made his teachings Christian knowledge…. Learning and teaching have both brought me peace and happiness…. Leave me my peace of mind! I refuse to look into that tube!"*

Galileo responds to his friend: *"But the truth, Cesare! The truth! Doesn't that mean anything?… To me peace and happiness have always meant one thing: to seek truth and admit what I found."*

According to our founding mothers and fathers, we are endowed with life, liberty, and the pursuit of happiness [via truth]. Like discovering that there's stardust all over creation, we might stumble into a new way of seeing things. We might have the audacity to look into that tube and see this brave new world for the first time. And we might just find out if pigs have wings.

6/9/2019

# Unwed Fathers

Back in the day, there used to be homes for unwed mothers. They were the results of a enigmatic condition called an unwanted pregnancy which always seemed the result of an accident. Back in those same days, teen pregnancy was considered a terrible sin of sorts which led half of the perpetrators to leave town for a while until the delivery was done. The unwed father was simply left alone and disgraced.

I remember vividly in my first parish when a sixteen-year-old was "sent away" to the nearest Florence Crittenton when her pregnancy was quite apparent. As her pastor, I was invited to conduct chapel one day. When I arrived, I was ushered into a large room with about sixteen pregnant teenagers in rocking chairs. I avoided the obvious pulpit and pulled up an extra rocker. In that congregation, I was helplessly without words so I asked the ladies in waiting to give me a few clues.

After a pregnant pause, somebody said "Please don't condemn us or make us feel any more guilty. We get enough of that." That's when I put away the Bible and notes and listened and learned. I had just graduated from seminary, but they had been to a school the likes of which I could never know, and they were faced with a dilemma that would have been the death of me. They were basically being forced to deliver their baby and place it up for adoption. They had no freedom of choice in the matter.

Their plights were forged by a two-edged sword. Pregnancy out of wedlock had condemned them to this gentle prison, and the concept of sex as the original sin became another whip to let them know that their pregnancy was God's punishment for their sin. What a theological mockery.

After several other incidents like that one, I became an advocate for the rights of women – young and old – to be able to make their own choice in such matters. After Roe v. Wade, clinics began to offer other healthy and civilized choices for these special people called "unwed mothers". Planned Parenthood offered much better alternatives to unplanned accidents.

Throughout this process, I tried to bring some comfort to the other partner in the process – not the crime! But there were never homes for unwed fathers.

6/16/2019

# Pursuit of Mediocrity

Spring. And for this young man sitting in a ninth grade English class, my fancy was heading off in many directions other than the pursuit of academic truth. The last class of the afternoon would soon be over, and we would all tear out of those halls of learning for whatever sport the day would bring. "Dudley," Mrs. Hart called, "would you read 'Thanatopsis' for the class." Shifting gears to the reality at hand, I stood at my desk and slowly began reading those dreadful words by William Cullen Bryant about dying. The poem seemed a mile long, but I made it through and took my seat once again.

"That was very mediocre," exclaimed the teacher.

"Thank you," I said in all innocence, for I had no earthly idea what she meant by that impressive word. She always used big words. There were giggles and snickers which were soon drowned by the bell and the shuffle of feet. Outside the door, several friends informed me of the true meaning of the word. And I have been fleeing it ever since so that, in the words of "Thanatopsis", " ..when thy summons comes to join / The innumerable caravan, that moves / To that mysterious realm, where each shall take / His chamber in the silent halls of death, / Thou go not like a quarry-slave at night."

In a recent column, the reemerging Garrison Keiller recalls a similar time: "When I was 16, Helen Fleischman assigned me to memorize Shakespeare's Sonnet No. 29, 'When in disgrace with fortune and men's eyes, I all alone beweep my outcast state,' for English class, and fifty years later, that poem is still in my head. Algebra got washed away, and geometry and most of biology, but those lines about the redemptive power of love in the face of shame are still here behind my eyeballs, more permanent than my own teeth."

At the heart of each of us is the desire to have significance. To be worth something. To be remembered. To make our mark on the world. And the way we go about it is in that mythical search for success through the pursuit of excellence. Maybe one of the reasons we pursue excellence is because we feel the hot pursuit of mediocrity at our heels. Thus, the chase for success is not just a running toward some kind of worth or significance; it is also a running away from the fear that we might be caught dead without having done a blooming thing right in our lives.

6/23/2019

# Self-Evident Truths

In declaring our independence from jolly old England several centuries back, the founding folk made a bold statement in the first sentence: "We hold these truths to be self-evident…" Little did they realize how sensitive truth would become in our day and time. While George Washington's never-tell-a-lie cherry tree incident might have gotten him elected, alternate political strategies have emerged in which white lies get the job done. It's hidden in plain sight, and it's as obvious as the nose on Pinocchio's face.

Underneath such an assumption was that some truths were more evident than others. While all men might have been created equal, it was understood that some were more equal than others. The word "men" excluded slaves, women and the kids which made keeping your *pluribus* more *unum*.

Underlying the rebellion that became the American Revolution was a trade war in which the mother country wanted more taxes for their blooming tea. Something greater was brewing beneath all that rhetoric, and that something had to do with freedom from the monarchy. The musical "Hamilton" gets at some of those larger issues going on then and now, like how it took a bunch of ragtag immigrants to get the job done. [There's a truth that might be offensive to some.]

By the way, truth and freedom very seldom coexist peacefully except over entrances to college buildings or in cross stitch notions like "You Shall Know the Truth, and the Truth Will Set You Free". Test that theory with Galileo's discovery of a very inconvenient truth that the earth really is not the center of the universe. Or issues surrounding gender inequality or global warming.

The God of Moses made several suggestions for how we ought to get along with each other, and one of those happened to mention something called bearing false witness. You should read the list of ten in the older testament and see how it might not be worthy of hanging up in a courtroom where people swear on an English King James Bible [where Jesus only spoke in red letters] to tell the truth.

You really can't make up this stuff, but you can easily put it in the basement in a box labeled "suspect notions that might come in handy later." Before you tape that box, you might want to put in some of the other idiosyncrasies of religions that seem to have their own corner on truth. Christians are the world's worst faith for inventing the world's best exaggerations. Just ask them how the earth was created. Or which denomination does God love best. Or why they think God meant for abortion to be the eleventh commandment. You know that the word "abortion" never appears in holy writ – neither in the infallible King James version nor fake editions.

Nobody in their right pew seems to remember Jesus' admonition about how all the nations will be judged: …for I was hungry and you gave me food, I was thirsty and you gave me something to drink, I was a stranger and you welcomed me, I was naked and you gave me clothing, I was sick and you took care of me, I was in prison and you visited me." Just before his untimely execution by the state, Jesus stands before Pilate and claims he has come to testify to the truth. And that's when the politician Pontius reacted with pious hubris and a rhetorical question: "What is truth?" Then went and washed hands of the whole thing.

If such self-evident truth be known, it would take an act of congress for those final words of Jesus of Nazareth to ever happen in our lifetime. Maybe that's why those first founders added an amendment to our constitution: *Congress shall make no law respecting an establishment of religion, or prohibiting the free exercise thereof.*

Honestly facing our pluralism and diversity, you begin to realize that maybe truth might not be that obvious since it is so ill-regarded. But we must not abandon the hope it can bring to a world honestly craving that magical peace that passes such understanding. We need to restore a time and place where middle school civics teachers, along with their students and parents, can watch the evening news without having to blush.

6/30/2019

# A Place Called Home

The good ol' summertime leads many of us down the primrose paths of vacations and travels to a variety of places all over the world. Or it might just be a short spin down memory lane to visit kith and kin. Suitcases, which were dormant during the winter, are filled to the brim with clothing and sundry other articles necessary for survival on the road. Cameras are loaded with fresh batteries, wallets with cash, cars washed, and houses tided in preparation for the long-awaited journeys. Time to leave what seems to be the ho-hum ordinariness of everyday life around the house and discover what's just beyond the blue horizon.

On the road and in the air, we're off to see whatever wizards of wonder we can discover at the beach or in the mountains or to the hinterlands of other continents. Some are even bold enough to travel to New Jersey to visit relatives! After a day or so of strange beds and showers, we experience this unconscious tug, this longing for the day when we will be back home. Such an experience does not negate the positive and new experiences we are enjoying. Not yet! But let the days pass and this strange illness develops within us. You don't need a physician to tell you that this is a case of homesickness.

Imagine what it must have been like for our pilgrim mothers and their husbands to have left their homeland or "mother" country to cast their lot in the new world. While the adventure must have had some invigorating aspects, there must have been this lurking desire to return to the familiar landscape of the old home place.

The children of Israel must have felt it out there in the forty-year wilderness, never mind the vision of the land filled with milk and honey. Homesick vagabonds following Moses to God knows where, almost willing to throw in the towel and go back to the known of Egypt's slavery.

But out there in the middle of nowhere, they learned this little trick that would stay with them for the rest of the Bible. They finally figured out that the only real home was the presence of God that seemed to be with them. In their writings they called God their "dwelling place". And somehow that realization created all the comforts of home for them wherever they might be on the road or however messy the tent became.

Perhaps another way of being at home in this world is to see the good Earth itself as the only home we have. While we may differ in so many aspects like continents or race or religion or nationality or income disparity, unless we find a way to live together in peace and harmony, we are all bound to live as aliens from some other planet. If we don't take care of each and ALL of us and this planet we inhabit, we are doomed to be among the homeless vagabonds wandering around forever.

7/7/2019

# The Energy of Expectations

When a fifteen-year-old tennis player ends up on center court at Wimbledon, she commands a fervor of respectful energy from the spectators in the stadium and on the screens in our dens. They can no longer just be spectators, because their hopes and dreams are pinned to this courageous would-be champion. Their expectations become the magic force of momentum felt by the young lady in tennis attire at the center of the world's best venue.

That's simply a snapshot of just how great expectations can be harnessed as a form of energy felt round the world. Some might call it "synergy" which Mr. Webster defines *as the benefit that results when two or more agents work together to achieve something either one couldn't have achieved on its own. It's the concept of the whole being greater than the sum of its parts.*

When I used to work for a living, I was hired to be a wordsmith of good news. Some referred to us as preachers of the word. For me, the most powerful force that kept me honed to the task of being honest to the pulpit was the realization that those in the pews that morning were half of the equation of the sermon. Early on and throughout my career, I was blessed by congregations who expected me to give them the very best I had to offer. Which meant creating the sermon, practicing it, rewriting and practicing until you would rise to their expectations. Week in and week out. Even if we disagreed on what I might have said, we always honored and respected each other as part of the Sunday morning equation where the whole experience was greater than the sum of its parts. And I had promised God and them that I would use all the "energy, intelligence, imagination and love" in doing my task. By the way, the "energy" for the pulpit came more from the pew side of the equation.

Even the ghosts of those dearly departed would haunt me to do my part of this endeavor as I had vowed to do. And I didn't want to mess with their sacred memories because their expectations of us all did not necessarily die with them. They had pinned their eternal hopes on the likes of us to keep this little church going strong 'til kingdom come.

While this concept applies to the corporate community, this same energetic creativity works within individuals. It is the old Pygmalion principle that brought life to the breathless statue, and it continues to breathe life into every person who is loved for the promise they show, no matter how low they may be or feel. In the musical "My Fair Lady", Eliza Doolittle is transformed by the belief of Henry Higgins. In the down-trodden flower peddler of Convent Garden, he saw the promise of something more. He staked his bet on that possibility he saw in her, and she won.

If you listen carefully, you can hear the same thing going on in the Bible. It is not so intent on getting people to believe in God or to trust in Jesus as it is in declaring that God believes in us. God sees something promising about us. More than a story of the faith of God's people, the Bible is a story of God's faith in all of us.

Our money is a form of energy. It represents our work and the energy we invested in that job. Whether we admit it or not, God also has some skin in that game, unless you believe you are a self-made person who accomplished everything by yourself, including the creation itself with all that infrastructure. The synergistic equation of all of this might require that we reprint our dollars to say "God Trusts in Us". And that affirmation of faith might give us all the courage we need to make this world a heavenly court made for champions of love who serve nothing less than the very finest to all God's people because God, our divine audience, has great expectations for us all.

7/14/2019

# A Man on the Moon

Superman was a superhero in my childhood days of yore. He could leap tall buildings with a single bound and travel places faster than a speeding bullet, unless someone hit him in the head with kryptonite. When Aunt Liba bought Superman capes for Ben, Jr. and me, we failed in our attempted flight from the roof of the garage. We did fly but did not prepare for so quick a landing. Mama's exclamatory disclaimer for such a venture: "you had no more business doing that than a man on the moon."

Little did she realize at that moment that her middle child would set his sight on that moon in more ways than one. Even though it was close to the geographic center of the sovereign state of Mississippi in the 1950's, Canton, Mississippi, was not necessarily the center of the universe when I was growing up there. Nor would it ever become so, contrary to some of its most prominent citizens. However, our back yard had enough night sky to make it seem like an observatory if not a planetarium, even to the naked eye searching for the naked truth. A neighbor stationed in Korea for the conflict sent me a celestial telescope, and I built a mount in the middle of that back yard. And that is where I could see the Soviet Union's Sputnik circling our American heavens in the October sky of 1957.

In 1960, I headed to college to become an astronomy major, not only because it was my passionate hobby, but because of the inspiring words of the young President who was elected in November of that year. While John F. Kennedy did not know where Canton might have been, there was one kid from there who became enamored with national politics because of him. And like a distant shepherd, he would lead me through the next three tumultuous years from his place in time and space.

*And so, my fellow Americans:* he said, *ask not what your country can do for you—ask what you can do for your country. My fellow citizens of the world: ask not what America will do for you, but what together we can do for the freedom of man...knowing that here on earth God's work must truly be our own.*

Speaking to the packed stadium at Rice University in Houston on September 12, 1962, the eloquent orator gave us a vision of a world beyond this one: *There is no strife, no prejudice, no national conflict in outer space as yet. Its hazards are hostile to us all. Its conquest deserves the best of all mankind, and its opportunity for peaceful cooperation may never come again.*

*We choose to go to the moon in this decade and do the other things, not because they are easy, but because they are hard, because that goal will serve to organize and measure the best of our energies and skills, because that challenge is one that we are willing to accept, one we are unwilling to postpone, and one which we intend to win, and the others, too....*

*And, therefore, as we set sail we ask God's blessing on the most hazardous and dangerous and greatest adventure on which man has ever embarked.*

And fifty years ago, **we** – in the finest meaning of that word – landed on that moon, and all of us could see ourselves and our spaceship Earth from space! The mission was accomplished and those early astronauts would take not only one but many steps and leaps for us all. To celebrate such an achievement, our oldest daughter landed on earth, July 19, 1969.

On November 22, 1963, two other college friends and I had driven up to Vanderbilt to look at attending their seminary. After a brilliant theologian thoroughly shocked and explained to us southern preacher wannabes how much thrust it would have taken for Jesus to leave the earth's gravitational field, we adjourned to the dining hall where the word came to us over the PA system: President Kennedy has been shot. Hunger left us completely as a funeral pall spread over the country and the world. The three of us simply and quietly got back in our car and drove the Natchez Trace to Jackson trying to find any am radio station for "further developments".

Listening back into that transforming moment, you can still hear faint radio signals, as if broadcasting from the moon itself: "Houston, Tranquility Bay here… the Eagle has landed." And when we reflect on what good has happened in those fifty years because of the high and holy hopes planted in the backyards of our existence, it can still take your breath away. We have been given the courage to fly with the same amount of reason as that of a man on the moon.

7/21/2019

# Outdoing Ourselves

It's one of those subtle terms we use to describe something in the superlative ranges of human behavior or achievement. It basically means to exceed or surpass the normally expected. It implies a sense of competition whereby someone outdoes the opponent in a particular feat. And when we speak of outdoing ourselves, we mean competing with self.

But the term really becomes a mixture of meanings at times. For instance, if you "outdo" yourself on something, does that mean that you are outdone? In the South, that particular term means that you are put out with someone. I can remember as a child that my mother became outdone with some of my mischievous achievements when I really outdid myself.

Most of us were brought up with the notion that we ought to better ourselves. Climb the ladder of success by trying not only to exceed the standards set by others but excelling over the standards we set for ourselves. Ambition is a very noble goal until it enters the realm of the problematic perfectionists who because they never can quite measure up to their own expectations, are forever frustrated with a feeling of incompleteness and failure. At some point in the quest to outdo ourselves, we come up to the wall and realize we can never be more than we are nor do more than we can do.

Human beings are limited creatures, bound by time and space and ability. When we say that we are <u>only</u> human, we are not so much admitting defeat as confessing our true situation. There's a limit to what we can do.

While I'm not a big believer in the doctrine of original sin [regular or crispy], at the heart of the biblical story is the notion that part of our problem is that we are trying to outdo ourselves and deceive ourselves into thinking that we are gods. From building the tower of Babel to keeping the Law perfectly, we human beings have been trying to outdo each other and ourselves in order to become God since day one. While it was called an original sin, it had devastating consequences. God became quite outdone with Adam and Eve's attempt to outdo themselves and did them in by running than out of the Garden.

So here we are, done in by the ancestors according to the oral tradition and all myths appertaining thereunto. In a dog-eat-dog world, everyone tries to outdo their neighbor. Even on a personal level, the competition becomes quite trite: trying to outdo ourselves can become our very undoing.

What's a person to do? Reinhold Niebuhr expressed the contradiction we feel when he prayed "O God, grant us the serenity to accept what cannot be changed, the courage to change what can be changed, and the wisdom to know the difference."

7/28/2019

# Shall We Dance?

Way back in my childhood hometown's quest to understand God and the religions of the world, the only real question that needed an answer from the Almighty was: Can Baptist dance? Obvious answer was…some can and some can't! Of course, they spent their youth groups figuring out just how dancing would lead down that slippery slope to sloppier sins that would give God hissy fits.

Dancers turn up in the strangest places in scripture. In Jeremiah's prophetic vision of Israel's return and restoration: *Then shall the maidens rejoice in the dance, and the young men and the old shall be merry. I will turn their mourning into joy.* Remember Miriam and the other ladies with tambourines dancing to praise the parting of the sea. David dancing without too much where-with-all before the ark of the covenant. For his birthday, Herod's niece danced before him, and John the Baptist lost his head – literally. Condemnation of dancing – dirty or otherwise – is conspicuously absent in holy writ.

Quite to the contrary, words come rolling out of scriptures that hit us right between the ears and down through the heart and straight to our feet almost demanding a dance: *Rejoice always, pray without ceasing, give thanks in all circumstances; for this is the will of God in Christ Jesus for you. Do not quench the Spirit… hold fast to what is good.* When we let these words become the meditations of our hearts, we just might feel the urge to *Dance, then, wherever you may be, I am the Lord of the Dance, said he, And I'll lead you all, wherever you may be, And I'll lead you all in the Dance, said he.*

47

All cultures of the earth have found the dance as a way of being in touch with a holiness beyond us and yet within us. For two summers at Camp Kickapoo, I was the Choctaw tribal dancer for Order of the Arrow ceremonies, wearing pretty much what David wasn't wearing when he danced that day. Those First American dances transcended the Mississippi mud on which I was dancing to the beat of a different drummer and led me into a form of mysticism beyond my Calvinistic upbringing.

Whirling dervishes perform a dance called the Sema, a religious dance performed to express emotion and achieve the wisdom and love of God. It originated in Turkey, in the in the mystical version of Islam known as Sufism. Here is a way of praying with abandon. Letting the holy lead you in sacred movement, like liturgical dance that became the rage in some Protestant churches in the 1970's?

Don't forget those words in Ecclesiastes: *A time to weep and a time to laugh; a time to mourn and a time to dance.* If we are not careful, dancing will lead us into all sorts of temptations, like laughing out loud for Christ's sake! This might be a good place to just use our common sense. William James warned us that *Common sense and a sense of humor are the same thing moving at different speeds. A sense of humor is just common sense, dancing.*

8/4/2019

# To Kill a Mockingbird

The only gun I own these days is a dead one. It's old and rusty and hangs on the wall in my study with a rose in the barrel. Walmart doesn't carry the ammunition for guns used in the recent war of northern aggression. In its day it did a lot of damage for a lost cause for which so many gave the last full measure of devotion and from which so many today will not get over. So the century and a half year old Springfield just hangs there passively remembering those dark days of aggressive slaughter in the hands of my great grandfather at Antietam and Gettysburg – a silent witness to what's gone with the wind.

The problem is that the problem of racism resulting from that irrepressible conflict way back then did not leave on those winds but has returned with a vengeance to haunt us and fill our headlines with the same old hate that uses assault machine guns and other military weapons to murder innocent children in their schools or people praying in their church or synagogue or mosque.

In the days of my sordid youth, guns were part of my hunting endeavors with Grandaddy and later with friends. The Boy Scouts taught us all the safety rules to earn a merit badge, but they also ask me to support an oath that included kindness and reverence for life. Southern ethics forbade the killing of innocent Mockingbirds. When our children were born and moved in with us for two decades, I gave up my right to bear arms and armed myself with a kinder, gentler spirit without a gun in sight except the deceased Springfield to remind us we lost that war anyway.

We live in a time and place that lets us enjoy life with liberty to pursue happiness. Somewhere along our common way, guns exploded into nothing short of weapons of mass destruction. Terrorists were no longer over yonder but right here among us. They were white Christians rather than Muslims. A "war on gun violence" becomes the current oxymoron while fear stalks our streets and classrooms looking for more innocent victims. Overkill becomes an understatement.

It's the perfect time for a come-to-Jesus moment, but we can't seem to shed our defensive attitudes long enough for that. Instead, we drag the Prince of Peace into the battle wondering just which weapon he would use. If we can't get a religious revival going, could we ask for an act of congress to rise up and resolve this national crisis before it becomes the death of us all. It would be a decent thing to do, but moral scruples are conspicuously absent from the body politic.

Maybe a scout could confront us with some simple American values of being trustworthy, courteous, kind, reverent and brave. Perhaps we can find folk with a different kind of intellectual and moral caliber — like Atticus Finch.

8/11/2019

# Here Be Dragons

Sometimes I depend on the handwriting on the walls to get my bearings each day. We have a clock that shines its information on our ceiling each night, giving us the time, the temperatures inside and outside. Those are important flat pieces of information to help me get my bearings as I go to sleep and when I wake.

Smelling the coffee sets off a cozy perspective that the divine has come down from heaven to our kitchen, and all is right with the world. So far. But then I read the newspaper, and everything goes out of whack. That's just small potatoes when it comes to really understanding our place not just in the kitchen, but in the family, in the community, in the world, and in the universe. Those venues are always changing and creating a kind of chaos in our attempt to know just who and where we might be at any given time.

That's when we could all use a personal and internal gyroscope, those little gizmos that airplanes and space stations utilize to keep their bearings as they speed through space. Prior to that, navigators used magnetic compasses, sextons and astrolabes to figure out where they might be upon the high seas at night. East and west you could sense during the daylight hours, but at night you were in the dark.

Central to night navigation was Polaris, the North Star. That was the one constant year-round; you could set your course by that. Of course, that was when the earth was flat as a pancake and set upon pillars above the deep. In 140 CE, Ptolemy had made his maps of the skies, and they were the gospel truth at the time. We were in a geocentric universe. Cartographers inscribed "Here Be Dragons" on the edges of the known flat world.

In 1540, Copernicus published his heliocentric theory of the universe, and about seventy years later Galileo uses his telescope to find that Jupiter had four moons, our moon had craters, and we were part of the Milky Way galaxy. Of course, he was condemned to hell and put under house arrest by the Church for daring to upset the holy perspective by Biblical proportions. Four hundred years later, in 2008, the Roman Catholic Church announced that it had made a mistake in condemning Galileo.

Moon landings, Hubble telescopes, and astrophysics have put a new twist on all our perspectives of just who and where we are in the cosmos. Carl Sagan's book **Pale Blue Dot** was inspired by an image taken by Voyager 1 in 1990. As the spacecraft left our planetary neighborhood for the fringes of the solar system, engineers turned it around for one last look at its home planet.

Just when we thought we had a handle on it, the pesky poet throws us a curve ball as drastic as the "Here Be Dragons" on the edge of flat earth maps: *When all the great galactic systems/ Sigh to a frozen halt in space/ Do you think there will be some remnant/ Of beauty of the human race/ Do you think there will be a vestige/ Or a sniffle or a cosmic tear/ Do you think a greater thinking thing/ Will give a damn that man was here?*

8/18/2019

# Risky Business

Seems like only yesterday when someone hauled my scrawny mind to the first grade, singing "School days, school days, dear old Golden Rule days..." That's when we all got our first Coca-Cola ruler with the Golden Rule written on it. Not only was I exposed to "reading and 'riting and 'rithmetic", but learning how to do unto others as you would want others to do unto you. Radical thought.

Education is risky business. Remember the adage "What they don't know won't hurt them"; the converse of that oversimplification might also apply. The process of learning is like a trek in the wilderness or like exploring unknown regions of questions we never thought about. When we discover the history of ideas or the intricacies of science or the imagination of math, our world grows larger and the landscapes of our lives take on new shapes. Education takes the idle mind, or the addle mind, or perhaps the most difficult of all, the narrow mind, and cultivates curiosity. And we all know what that did to the proverbial cat!

At the heart of it, the scriptures tell of humankind learning: learning the Torah, or the Wisdom, or listening to the parables of a rabbi from Nazareth who was dead set on teaching folk about the wonders of God's love and the responsibilities we are to enjoy in this Kingdom in the midst of us. It was marvelous, of course, his teaching. Too much so. Too good to be true. Too close to home. Too risky.

"Teacher", asked one of his hearers, "What must I do to have eternal life?" And the teacher offered a course on Golden Rule type neighborly love through a simple parable. The problem was that too many people found Samaritans [today he might just as well say

Palestinians or immigrants] so offensive that they dropped out of the course and tried to figure out ways to discredit the rabbi or to shut down his roving schoolhouse. It wasn't that he was teaching anything new, or talking out of school; he was reminding them of the stuff in their own book, which obviously they had failed to understand. They got mad as hell at him one day for his including non-Jews in his lessons that they threatened to hurl him off the nearest cliff.

At the end of Deuteronomy, Moses wraps up his teaching career with the children of Israel with a beautiful image: "May my teaching drop as the rain, my speech distills as the dew, as the gentle rain upon the tender grass, and as the showers upon the herb." When we open ourselves to the possibilities of daring to be well-educated people, our parched minds and souls can grow some of the most outlandish things, especially some wild thoughts about ourselves and this world in which we live. We might even learn at last to love God with all our minds and our neighbors as ourselves. Or the Golden Rule. Education is risky business. But so is living.

8/25/2019

# Trivial Pursuits & Idle Conversations

The Calvinistic work ethic that so many of us Protestants seemed to have inherited from God knows where [and I hope God knows why!] makes us suspect of people who would engage – or even think about it – in trivial pursuits or idle conversations. According to this inbred doctrine, we must spend our lives in an orderly pursuit of worthwhile goals. We should always work like the devil to produce results that are clearly measurable and have some utilitarian purpose.

In my collegiate years, Florence Nightingale pinpointed this notion and grabbed my work-ethic imagination with a quote that hung on my dorm wall: *Live your life while you have it. Life is a splendid gift. There is nothing small in it. For the greatest things grow by God's Law out of the smallest. But to live your life you must discipline it. You must not fritter it away in "fair purpose, erring act, inconstant will" but make your thoughts, your acts, all work to the same end and that end, not self but God. That is what we call character.*

While those words might have kept my shoulder to the wheel, nose to the grindstone, and midnight oil burning in that old dorm room, it's beginning to occur to me in the latter phases of my years, that there just might be some merit in whiling away time in things that seem insignificant and spending more energy on less energetic endeavors. Of course, that's easier said than done. Given our modus operandi, we'd have to be sure everything else was done before we could really enjoy such slack occasions.

When you read the accounts of Jesus in the gospels, there is an apparent easy-going and laid-back manner that he uses to disarm people while disturbing their spirits. There is a certain degree in which the rabbi sees a larger truth in what others might call trite: a latent mustard seed full of possibilities; salt that's worth more than its salt. A pearl worth more than life itself. Birds of the air. Lilies of the field that toil not nor spin but which outdo Solomon in all his accomplishments. Who in the world has time to be provoked by such trivial things? It's like stumbling over stardust.

E.B. White once quipped that when got up every morning, he was "torn between a desire to improve the world and a desire to enjoy the world. This makes it hard to plan the day."

Maybe one of the best gospels we can hear is that it's OK to pursue the insignificant delights and enjoy idle chatter about nothing in particular. To stop and smell the roses and feast upon the stars. I don't mean to become lackadaisical or languid or lazy; nor do I intend that we approach everything with nonchalance or complacency.

Every splendid inch of living is a gift outright – neither earned nor created by the likes of us – and a passion for this beautiful life requires a quiet enjoyment of simple pleasures and easy-going pastimes. Maybe we should work on that more!

9/1/2019

# You Don't Know Me

"You don't know who I am, do you?" That's the way she put the question to me at a recent gathering. I honestly did not know how to answer her question. For the life of me I could not put a name on her face. I did remember having met her several years ago. Not sure where or when. My mind worked rapidly but to no avail. She was standing there with her question in front of me: "You don't know who I am, do you?"

Inside, I was dealing with embarrassment. My good ol' sense of inadequacy rose up in me like the sun in the morning and the moon at night. Shame on me for not being able to recall the name of this woman or remember where or when we had met. I shuffled my feet, looked at the floor, trying to find an exit. Maybe she would walk away and take her question with her: "You don't know who I am, do you?"

The moment of truth was there. Fish or cut bait. The ball was roundly in my square court, so I answered her question quite simply: "Yes." The answer was as oblique as the question. But she had put it to me as a "yes or no" proposition. "Yes", I said, leaving her to fill in "I don't know you."

Should I blame my faux pas on the tendency of the aging process to forget? Perhaps it's just a human thing. The mind simply goes blank; the computer's memory chip fails us at times. The tip of my tongue can get very crowded at times.

Preacher Gordon was an erudite bachelor minister in the last generation of the great southern Presbyterian saints and overly admired by the single ladies of his congregations. In his later years he was invited to preach at a former parish. As he was shaking hands after the service, this woman grabbed his hand and exclaimed, "I bet you don't remember me." Without so much as a pregnant pause, Gordon replied, "When I left here, darling, I had to forget you in order to get on with my work."

Mary Magdalene was up early on that first day of the week, according to John's Easter Gospel. When she found the tomb empty, she was beside herself. Someone, whom she mistook to be a gardener, asked her about her troubled look. The conversation is Jesus's way of saying to Mary "You don't know who I am, do you?" For the life of her, she couldn't figure out this stranger of Galilee who dared us to welcome the stranger. Honor all people. Love your neighbor and your enemy. Wait! Did the Jesus say "enemy"? That's pushing the envelope. Maybe the rabbi had heard the old Jewish proverb that says "my enemy is just a person whose story I haven't heard yet."

We've heard the old, old stories of Jesus forever, but we still have an identity crisis recognizing him in our neighbors and enemies. In true Matthew 25 form, we could ask *when did we see you a stranger and welcomed you, or naked and give you clothing?* And the all-inclusive answer, of course...*just as you did it to one of the least of these...!*

9/8/2019

# Bible Verses

Before the world was coming to its end in the year 2000, remember when it was quite commonplace to see someone holding a big sign in the football stadium forthrightly proclaiming "JOHN 3:16"? Most folk could easily fill in the blank beginning with...*for God so loved the world*...etc. The real implication was that if you did not know Jesus, it's adios!

The whole idea of the bible is derived from the Greek word for books, and it is full of many "books". Books are divided into chapters, and chapters into verses. Regard for this book of books varies from the die-hard "The Bible says it; I believe it; case closed" to "who thought up this unbelievable stuff"?

To contribute to the confusion, I thought it might be somewhat ungodly to give it a go here in the blogosphere and to write like I was writing bible verses to add gravitas to these words of my mouth and the meditations of my heart. There's no leather cover or golden edges, and I will not speak in red. We'll call this book Stumbling Over Stardust...or SOS for short. [That's the same for Song of Solomon, so don't get confused]. This issue is the 28th one, so we will call this...

*Stumbling Over Stardust, Chapter 28* *¹When I was a kid, bible verses were the cat's meow in Sunday School. ²We had to memorize them and then use them to answer the roll call. Of course, everybody's favorite verse was "Jesus wept." ³It was so memorable. First one called used that one, and the rest of us scrambled for the favorite leftovers.*

*⁴I threw a kink in the system one Presbyterian sabbath morning by quoting some obscure ditty from the KJV: "Let love be without*

dissimulation, abhor that which is evil; cleave to that which is good."
[Romans 12:9] [5]A silent pall fell over the class; they were either mysti-
fied, mortified or horrified that I had dare use an unknown five-syl-
lable word from scripture along with verbs like "abhor" and "cleave"
in order to account from my presence.

[6]Using any other version of the bible was frowned upon, but
had I been able to I could have quoted from the RSV – "Let love be
genuine; hate what is evil, hold fast to what is good" – but it would
have been far less confounding and mysterious.

[7]Holy writ has been so overly misused that's it's hard to remember what the writers' had in mind to begin with. [8]Some Presbyterians
thought and taught that God Himself [or Herself... that's another
chapter] wrote these words while holy men sedated by the spirit were
mere conduits for these final scripture verses. [9]Having grown up as
a naive Sunday schooler who blindly learned so many verses "by
heart", I was blown away when I took a college course utilizing the
form critical method of understanding scriptures and translated this
stuff from the original languages in seminary.

[10]When all of the convictions and confinements of the Bible
were put in their proper places, this book of books became at last the
Good Book I had imagined and worshiped. [11]It's quite a relief not to
have to speak in verses or live by John 3:16 alone. [12]And I'm free to
understand that the ordinary men and women who wrote all those
books and chapters and verses were ordinary people whose lives were
committed to making sure these old, old stories kept going through
ordinary people like us.

You can take my word for it: this isn't necessarily the word of God. Thanks be to God.

9/15/2019

# Cowboys and Angels

Ken Burns' PBS series on *Country Music* raised our awareness of a particularly American genre of music. I've always loved the stuff for it's downright affable and laughable way of portraying despair and desperation. Just take a couple of tell-all titles: "How Can I Miss You, If You Won't Leave?" or "If the Phone Don't Ring, It's Me!"

Justin and Ryan Harris grew up right here in West End and are currently making quite a name for themselves on the Nashville music scene. They call themselves "McKenzies Mill", taken from their name of the road where they lived as young boys. When they made their first album called *One Hell of a Ride*, their proud father Ricky slipped me a copy with this warning: "Preacher, this ain't church music!" After listening to it, I took it back and let him know that "there's more church music here than in church most Sundays."

Someone defined country music as being just three chords and the truth. And if you knew where to tune your pickup's radio a while back, you could catch Garth Brooks singing a tender melody about cowboys and angels that brought pathos to your soul if not tears to your eyes.

The song begins on the eighth day of creation when God realized that a cowboy could never make it on his own. So *"God took passion and thunder, patience and wonder, then sent down the best thing that God ever made...."* Then comes the chorus: *Cowboys and angels, leather and lace; Salt of the earth meets heavenly grace. Cowboys and angels, tested and tried; It's a long way to heaven, but one hell of a ride!*

While Garth is not purported to be a theologian, some of his tunes do take on an air of transcendence with a touch of incarnation. His mellow voice sings a higher form of the gospel truth than he may realize as he uses the heaven-on-earth metaphors as a way of portraying genuine human affection. He even touches the hearts of the more finely sophisticated among us with his down-to-earth phrases. And while it may not be a familiar hymn of praise, it is a song of faith freshly aired which touches a chord of passion that runs clear back to Eden.

One of the most powerful ways we experience the love of God is in the mystery of that very human love between a man and a woman – a cowboy and an angel. And for generations, poets and song writers, artists and composers, have tried to demonstrate how this love is part of a creative force beyond earth's domain. Maybe that's why, when they were trying to decide which books to keep in the canon of our scripture, a bunch of saintly men [perhaps with a few would-be cowboys in pickups] said emphatically, "The Song stays!" The Song of Songs, of course. Another love song where earlier salt of the earth met the same heavenly grace.

9/22/2019

# The World's Worst

Someone should have started a book long ago entitled "The World's Worst". Like Guinness describing the most and best, this tome would list the things at the other end of the spectrum. Surely, there's a list somewhere. Perhaps Dickens cataloged them in an undiscovered appendix to his novel idea: "It was the best of times; it was the worst of times.

Ever since I was knee high to a grasshopper, I heard that term used about all kind of folk for all kinds of situations. "Why, she's the world's worst when it comes to keeping her house clean", or "He's the world's worst golfer". Certainly, this is only a generic disclaimer; these folks are not the world's worst whatever. How in the world would you prove such a proposition? Even at a deeper level, when we've wronged someone, we say to ourselves or a close friend "I feel like the world's worst person for what I did". The feeling is usually authentic, and we try to find some way to make amends and restore ourselves at least to the world's average person — maybe even to slightly better than average.

Why do we do such a thing? Is it a way of getting off the hook or justifying ourselves and our mistakes? Theologians might say that this is simply acknowledging our "sinful nature, prone to evil". But it is never meant to reflect such a deep notion. It is more relativistic. It's our way of sizing up a situation with respect to our fellow human beings. We cozy up to the notion that grace means that God grades on a curve, and while we may be horrible at some aspect of life, we are basically decent people with a few minor faults. Compared to others, we feel fairly good about ourselves.

This is where the water hits the wheel when Jesus shows up with a new ethic where every person should be loved, respected and honored as the world's finest child of God. Did that ever set off a religious time bomb among the spiritually elite who used their religious supremacy to look down on those "others" whom they deemed the world's worst! Jesus himself would end up in the scope of their righteous rifles and soon be nailed to a cross between two of the world's worst criminals.

P. Buckley Moss, the artist of the Amish in the Shenandoah Valley, expresses this consternating contradiction when she paints this little girl praying these words above her: *Dear God, please make the bad people good and the good people easier to live with.*

9/29/2019

65

# For Pity's Sake

It's a very fragile word in the English language and can fall from the fence of meaning in two directions. There is a trite and trivial use of the word "pity", or there is the extremely noble quality of human compassion. Like its Latin root, <u>pietas,</u> or piety, it can cut both ways. We can mean by piety that a person is syrupy sweet, or we can understand that a person's authenticity is deeply rooted in a faith that illuminates the darkness with a greater source of meaning.

I recently heard a group of people describing a little get-together as a small "pity party" in which everyone sat around and played the old human game of "ain't it awful" and cried in their beer. Children learn at an early age how to play the pitiful game to elicit attention — and then play it the rest of their lives. Others despise being on the receiving end of pity, not wanting the sympathy vote in order to win anything from anyone. Remember beleaguered and pathetic Job in the old testament whose friends came with a form of pity salted with piety that sounded like they were at least one-up on their suffering crony and would not take pity on him for his plight. With friends like these, who needs enemies.

Something's happening to pity in our culture, and that's a crying shame. It's being erased or covered over. Or perhaps it's being manipulated in some ways. Whether it's wars or natural disasters or refugees with images coming into our dens every night, there's a distance created from their hurts and our hearts. We have become almost immunized against what seems the tyranny of pity and there's hardly a merciful bone in our bodies anymore.

In his most powerful parable to summarize the gospel truth, Jesus talks about the victim on the roadside who was passed over by the pious priest and the law-abiding Levite. *But a Samaritan while travelling came near him; and when he saw him, he was moved with pity.* What a simple Sunday School lesson to learn by heart and apply to the current needs staring us in the face.

Remember the rabbi's sermon on the mount: *Blessed are the merciful, for they shall receive mercy...*a sentiment echoed in Portia's appeal to Shylock in the *Merchant of Venice*:

> *The quality of mercy is not strained.*
> *It droppeth as the gentle rain from heaven*
> *Upon the place beneath. It is twice blest:*
> *It blesseth him that gives and him that takes.*

10/6/2019

# Assisted Living

Wikipedia defines it as "extra-care housing or retirement living which allows residents over 55 or 60 to live independently... with staff on hand 24 hours a day to provide personal care. Assisted living exemplifies the shift from 'care as service' to 'care as business' in the broader health care arena predicted more than three decades ago."

Right after my birth, I entered the assisted living home operated by my parents. They fed me and changed my diapers. They healed my illnesses and provided clean sheets and towels. Lots of free advice. When I was three, Mama's father came to live with us as another person needing assisted living until he died in the back bedroom when I was seven. I assisted in his death by sitting at his bedside for what seemed like forever because I still remember it as if it were yesterday.

My grandmother on Daddy's side, who assisted my birth as midwife, had a kindergarten in her home and helped over two dozen of us each day get ready for primary school. From grades one to twelve, some of the most noble teachers incorporated assisted living principles to help us get ready for "independent living".

But I have yet to experience such a thing. Even after college and graduate school and launching into a career, in every place of my life, I have always been dependent on so many other people or institutions to become me, myself and I. Now in the autumn years, I feel even more intertwined in the family and community that assists my free-range living every day of my life. And if it weren't for taxes and government spending where would we be: no education, no medical care, no defense, no clean air, no roads.

Our living is always assisted to the extent that there's not a single self-made independent person anywhere.

When Grandaddy died in the back bedroom, I was there holding his frail hand. I felt the life going out of him. My first experience of assisted dying. One of his favorite phrases was "much obliged", and that term captures our lifetimes of gratitude for all those who assisted us and helped us on the journey as a way of keeping the circle unbroken from generation to generation.

10/13/2019

# Original Sin

It's a subject that's always been dear to my heart and confounding to my mind. Lawrence Raab, the New England poet about my age says it so well I'd like to dive into this ubiquitous subject with his words:

*That was one idea my mother*

*always disliked. She preferred her god*

*to be reasonable, like Emerson or Thoreau*

*without their stranger moments.*

*Even the Old Testament God's*

*sudden angers and twisted ways*

*of getting what he wanted she'd accept*

*as metaphors. But original sin*

*was different. Plus no one agreed*

*about whether it was personal, meaning*

*all Adam's fault, or else some kind*

*of temporary absence of the holy,*

*which was Adam's fault as well.*

*In any case, it made no sense*

*that we'd need to be saved before*

*we'd even had the chance*

*to be wrong. Yes, eventually everyone*

*falls into error, but when my sister and I*

*were babies she could see we were perfect,*

*as we opened our eyes and gazed up at her*

*with what she took for granted as love,*

*long before either of us knew the word*

*and what damage it could cause.*

During my many ages of innocence, I was often perplexed by how sin became so original from the outset of creation. When I was at some pre-cognizant stage of development, Mamaw, my dear grandmother, carefully taught me the Children's Westminster Catechism. Even though you might have no earthly idea of being conscious of such questions, they seemed to be important to adults at the time for a kid like me to learn them "by heart".

While the first group of questions came with nifty answers about the nature of God, Question 28 asks point blank *What is sin? The answer, of course, was Sin is any want of conformity unto, or transgression of the law of God.* Question 35 wants to know *What effect had the sin of Adam on all mankind?* The less-than-obvious answer was *All mankind are born in a state of sin and misery.* [or as Adam exclaimed after eating the apple: I'll be damned!] And for the bonus, this leads immediately to Question 36 *What is the sinful nature which we inherit from Adam called?* **Original Sin.**

Over my many miles as a pastoral pilgrim, this old notion had a hard time cutting muster with me. Even after studying the scriptures and enough books to become a resident theologian and minister, my experiences in life and work would not confirm any of this. Maybe it's my naivete of believing with Ann Frank: *I keep my ideals, because in spite of everything I still believe that people are really good at heart.*

This doctrine has led the downfall of many a good man, and I, O Lord, am just one who wonders why we have to start off in the red, like owing my soul to the company store [to quote Tennessee Ernie]. What if we were all born even and didn't have to spend our time and energy getting out of disgrace? What if goodness rather than sin's curse were a pre-existing condition? For these and many other questions with scant answers, stay tuned.

[To be continued]

10/20/2019

# God Is Not Mad at Us

[part two of *Original Sin*]

Should you have had the misfortune of attending worship in Northampton, Massachusetts in the summer of 1741, the sermon by Rev. Jonathan Edwards would have hit you like a ton of bricks. The title alone would have scared the holy hell out of any hearer: "Sinners in the Hands of an Angry God".

You might be dismissive of such a farfetched idea, thinking it from so far back in olden times that it lacks gravitas today. But if you look and listen, that same God seems to be alive and well and easily angered by our slightest inclination toward evil. Cathedrals are full of art works depicting the final judgement with the saved heading to heaven and the damned doomed to the inferno. Fear is the force at work in the sermon, the works of art, and the whole notion of original sin.

If this primary doctrine is to lead us to believe that we came into this world as pond scum or a lowly worm, that means we start off with a negative factor and spend our lives trying to get out of this infernal debt before we end up in hell. Such a doctrine needs to have subsequent doctrine that will lead Jesus to pay the price for my atonement. Believe it or not, the Church just happened to have a atonement dogma or two that brought in new members by the droves. Isaac Watts' hymn sings it like this: *Alas, and did my Savior bleed?/ And did my Sovereign die?/ Would He devote that sacred head/ For such a worm as I?* [That term "worm", always made me wonder that if God's eye is on the sparrow, who's watching the early bird?]

This personal Savior version of Jesus is the only gospel some people hear and believe in order save their own hides, to get the hell out of here and the devil take the hindmost. And even if Jesus paid it all, "love so amazing, so divine, demands my life, my soul, my all." In other words, I'm up to my neck in debt and in the red all over again.

Franciscan monk, Richard Rohr, puts it this way: *For some reason, most Christian theology seems to start with Genesis 3—which features Adam and Eve—what Augustine would centuries later call "original sin." When you start with the negative or with a problem, it's not surprising that you end with Armageddon and Apocalypse. When you start with a punitive, critical, exclusionary God, it's not surprising that you see the crucifixion as "substitutionary atonement" where Jesus takes the punishment that this angry God intended for us.*

That seems sufficient to many folks who just want to be saved, and let the rest of the world just go hang. If, however, you open up to rabbi Jesus as our teacher who urges us away from self-centered attempts to save ourselves and shows us how give ourselves away for the common good of all. Then, this sordid notion of personal salvation evaporates when he urges us to see the good in others…to see God in the faces of all our neighbors even as we do in ourselves. To take up the cross and follow him to heaven knows where. To consider the lily. To open the pearl of great price. To find treasure in a field. To love our enemies. To live lavishly like the daughters and sons of the prodigal father who loves all of us dearly.

Paul Scherer, one of the great preachers at the beginning of the last century, summarizes such a gospel like this: "Love is a spendthrift, leaves arithmetic at home, is always 'in the red!' And God is love!"

# Messing with the System

When this particular Sunday morning started coming down, you might have noticed you were off an hour, or at least your clocks were. And sooner or later, somebody's got to pay the piper for what's affectionately known as Daylight Saving Time by falling back. Mickey's big hand gets to go back one full circle, and you just got a one-hour bonus for this all-day extravaganza!

In case you haven't noticed, we live in a fairly dependable natural order thanks to that lucky old sun that rolls around heaven all day. But this solar system just didn't happen overnight; it took days – if not eons – to perfect. So what's an hour or two among friends, you might be asking. You've got all day to enjoy your extra hour or get over it. And then next spring you will lose it again. Like clockwork!

In spite of all our brilliance, I somehow feel that Mother Nature in not overly impressed with our temporal ingenuity as if we might somehow cheat her out of some time. She's already having a hissy fit when it comes to climate change and our lack of stewardship. This is no way to take care of the only spaceship we have to make it to nowhere in particular while we roll around heaven all day. Just another way of our messing up the system.

Many moons ago, I went to college to become an astronomer in order to help us win the space race during the Cold War. Time was a very important commodity in our calculations back before computers, satellites and atomic clocks. In the observatory we depended on the official time to be signaled via the Naval Observatory from Washington via shortwave radio.

For our final exam we had to compute the position of a particular star to be at a certain place at a certain time based on our latitude and longitude. We used a book called an ephemeris to give the trajectory of an astronomical object and slide rules to work out the calculations. For less than noble reasons, I chose a star that would be directly overhead at 9:04:36 CST.

The dome was closed, and the telescope's right ascension and declination were set on the prescribed position for the star in question. The short wave beeped the time signals from the Naval Observatory, and when the precise moment arrived the gears that drive the scope to follow a star were engaged. The dome was opened. If my star was in the telescope, I got an A; if not, I got an F.

The astronomy professor was rather short and stout to the extent he couldn't bend over low enough to look into the eyepiece to see my beautifully centered overhead star. He had to take my word for it as if I were in charge of the stars that were directly overhead that Mississippi evening. That's when I discovered that Jimmy Cricket was right about wishing upon a star!

Since then, I've resisted messing with the solar system except in those semiannual moments when I have to reset the clocks.

11/3/2019

# The Persimmon Tree

If you know what you're looking for, the persimmon trees will be bearing their fruit throughout the southeast in the coming weeks. In season October through February, persimmons are the golden delicious fruits that hang off the trees after the leaves drop in autumn. Often referred to as "the fruit of the Gods" but you have to wonder what on earth must have possessed the Creator to include the persimmon tree in the flora and fauna of creation? Of what use is it? What would have happened, for instance, if it had been the tree in the Garden of Eden out of which the snake had slithered? Had Eve taken one bite of that persimmon, she would never have been tempted to offer the thing to Adam. Sin itself might have become dormant because the persimmon lacks the delectability necessary for temptation and lacks the "core" value of the apple.

Or does it? It looks alright among the branches or on the ground, favoring the appearance of a nice-sized plum. But if you eat it in the raw, the only temptation that comes over you is to gag. Lips and mouth shrivel. Your teeth ache. Unlike the apple that's juicy to its very core, the persimmon will force the eater to think undignified thoughts and act in uncouth ways to get rid of the blooming thing. Maybe the Creator put that thing in the Garden on the first Halloween: the first treat that turned out to be a trick!

Maybe the persimmon is a symbol of another kind of sin which is not represented by the apple. Apple-like sins are those that are subtler, and on the whole, easy to live with. You nibble your way along, not doing the things you ought to do. You find yourself actually comfortable with coveting your neighbor's Mercedes. In a consumer-oriented, advertising-driven society like ours, we lust for the juices of plush lifestyles. Even TV evangelists who used to preach that you had to give up the world to save your soul are now pushing the notion that if you save your soul, then you will get the whole world. Just like the calf, the golden apple of opportunity tastes sweet to the rotten core.

Persimmon sins, on the other hand, backfire. These are the kind that look harmless and tempting, but as soon as you take the first bite you know you've messed up. The flashing blue light in the rear-view mirror signals within you an instant sickness that you broke one of the local commandments. You speak a small lie about a neighbor and later that afternoon she's on the phone to you. You react with a short fuse with one of your children and find it difficult to shave because you don't want to look at the sourpuss in the mirror.

Life is full of sweet and sour sins. We've tried some of each and ended up with persimmon on our breath. Forgive my far-fetched attempt to add another symbol to the already over-crowded Garden, but I still wonder why the Creator invented the persimmon. Maybe there was the possibility that at some time in the history of the universe, a few good people could turn that thing into something as marvelous as persimmon pudding with dollop of whipped cream and a hint of almond that occasionally graces the desert table at a church covered-dish supper. Maybe we will be known by our fruits, after all!

11/10/2019

# The Gravity of Maturity

When old Isaac Newton settled under that apple tree to discover gravity in the late 1600's, he had no earthly idea of the consequences of such a magic moment on the writing and reading of these words on this page right now. As my life continues to ripen, I have developed a few theories of my own about the core values of more than just an ordinary apple and less than the rocket science it might take to get my sorry older self in orbit around the moon if not to the celestial city when it comes my turn to shuttle off this mortal coil.

During the first half of our lives, we hardly notice the force of gravity because we are so energized and invigorated in pursuing success and raising families, that we dare not feel such a fearsome force. Besides, gravity is our friend that keeps our feet planted on the earth while our heads and hearts explore other parts of our existence.

Like so many other unseen wonders, the passage of time is something to which we seldom pay heed. But just like gravity, the steady march of time calls us forward relentlessly and, if like the

23rd psalmist we are lucky enough, we'll always have goodness and mercy tagging along. As you come around the final curves heading toward the finish line, you feel the gentle force get heavier with each step and each day. Sunrise, sunset, swiftly flow the years…one season following another…laden with happiness and tears and a tad more gravity.

During the first half of our lives, we are hell bent of doing our best to be as successful as we possibly can. In the latter half, "Staying Alive!" becomes our theme song.

A friend of mine took great delight in calling me once a year before seven o'clock in the morning to exclaim with charming surprise: "Dudley, I woke up with a seventy-two-year-old woman in my bed!" Year by year, it was the same message about the same woman with one more year added. I was glad to get the call just to know that the caller and the object of his affection were both alive! That's miracle enough. Then, as year gave way to year, they added depth to the phrase "until death do we part" which was the ultimate in human gravitas.

At the end of his poem "Reluctance", Robert Frost adds these befitting and poignant words:

> *Ah, when to the heart of man*
> *Was it ever less than a treason*
> *To go with the drift of things,*
> *To yield with a grace to reason,*
> *And bow and accept the end*
> *Of a love or a season?*

11/17/2019

# Inheriting the Earth

This new country was started with refugees daring to get in those little ships and set sail to a whole new world. As early as 1584 a group of English immigrants landed Roanoke Island. The settlement became known as the Lost Colony for obvious reasons, but Virginia Dare became the first "anchor baby" American.

The first Americans...aka the Native Americans...had lax immigration laws and were a bit perturbed about the idea that their land had not only been "discovered" by the paleface but was shortly occupied by a group known as the colonist...aka pilgrims...aka the founding mothers and their husbands... as if native mothers and fathers did not count because they had been here for generations.

Thanksgiving usually calls us to look back in time to remember the coming of the founding folks, portrayed in that poetic moment in grammar schools around the country when they broke bread together. In a few years they'd be breaking promises and breaking hearts as the white immigrants started grabbing hunks of what they thought was their God-given land and running those first Americans down a trail of tears and further into whatever wastelands could be created for them.

Over the years since then, wave upon wave of immigrants – including our own forebears – have come here expecting some land of their own. From England and Germany...Israel and Ireland... Poland and Paraguay...from Africa and Australia...from Mexico and Peru... We came from all over and somehow room was always found for another mouth to feed...a family to live...a house to be built. We were the folk of many faiths worshipping a variety of gods and thanking those very gods for a country like this one that gave us the freedom to worship as we will. What an inheritance to treasure…our God-given heirloom spinning in space.

In the final analysis, the Psalmist just might have a point…" the earth is the Lord's." We are merely inheritors from previous generations and have the responsibility of leaving the place in good shape for the generations yet to come. It's a kind of progressive thing…a movable feast almost. And the dinner guests are simply poor wayfaring strangers…traveling not only through this world but sojourners on the spaceship Earth.

Whether we are dirt poor or filthy rich, our lives themselves are simply gifts, part of the inheritance. We need to understand the global picture, but we need to act locally and responsibly and respectfully and lovingly…taking care of all our neighbors…be they foe or friend because they are also inheritors of this time and space. We must turn away from the greed to grab all we can that guides so much of our national and individual lives in order to share the inheritance: God's earth with all God's children.

11/24/2019

# Minding Your O's

As Christmas looms larger on our horizons, we might discover some childhood urge to behave or improve our attitudes. When I was a kid, we took seriously the musical admonition warning us to "...watch out, you better not cry...you better not pout, 'cause I'm telling you why..." Santa Clause, etc. Legends abounded about "ashes and switches and bow-legged britches." And the big boy down the street who wrote dirty words on the sidewalk, put away his chalk come early December. We all began to faithfully mind our parents and our manners during that season.

It was similar to the fear instilled in me when I attended worship before my feet could touch the floor below my pew. We always sat right behind Mrs. Mansell and just in front of Jesus holding his lamb in the stain glass window. During the winter, Mrs. Mansell always wore her two-headed fox fur stole with those beady black eyes staring right at me, daring me to make a move. The fear of God couldn't hold an advent candle to that scary sabbath circumstance.

That's where and when I discovered the imaginative allure to get your mind off the things going on around you. You had to invent stuff to change your mindfulness in the moment. I found that the church bulletin was a veritable playground without foxes or shepherds. After drawing doodles, I discovered the other art of using the little golf pencil to fill in the big O's. Then, I would go on to the little o's. If I really got scared or bored, I would attack the big D's. I was minding my manners and minding Mama by simply minding my O's.

It was like minding your P's and Q's, the warning issued by British pub owners just before closing time. Mind your pints and quarts and finish drinking so we can close the joint. In the back pews of the church, I'd be closing down my O's before the benediction. To get ready to outrun the lady with foxes on her shoulder. To look back at Jesus the shepherd until we would all meet again.

While my holy O endeavor was spiritual in nature, there was a practical outcome from the exercise: you would be prepared to take the SAT exam by filling the 0's with a #2 pencil.

12/1/2019

# The Singing Christmas Tree

When I was a mere child, the Canton Presbyterians prided themselves on their music programs for the children of the church. Beginning as Cherubs in the singing Christmas tree, we climbed our way through the musical scales to fortissimo in the Junior Choir, led and conducted by our only bachelor preacher, Dr. Charles R. McCain. Doc also played the piano while forcing our small voices to come forth with strange sounds called new hymns.

Others had taught us the great old songs for kids like "Climb, Climb Up Sunshine Mountain," "Jesus Loves Me," and "If the Devil Doesn't Like It, He Can Sit on a Tack". Doc took us on adventure treks through the big blue hymnal full of oblivious songs even for the adult choir. I distinctly recall our dozen or so songsters sitting on the front row of wooden chairs in the sanctuary annex straining to sing "The Lone Wild Fowl in Lofty Flight", which was chalked up as too difficult even for us.

When I was still in the Children's Cherubs, someone built a rather large green plywood frame in the shape of Christmas tree with six or seven rows rising from the widest at the floor level to only one step wide enough to hold our gauze-winged angel topper. We practiced our carols, and the night for the "Living Christmas Tree" finally arrived. Following our only golden haloed angel, the rest of us in white robes with red bows filed into our descending rows, and I ended up mid-tree to the utmost right of that row. I was only three or four feet off the floor as I gazed righteously at all those grownups who came to be put in the season's reason by our heavenly carols.

As the congregation quieted in anticipation for our performance, Bobby Heath, who was just behind me, uttered blasphemy in the congregation: "Dudley farted!" His words were picked up by all the cherubs and those in the first pews, and a hefty guffaw rumbled throughout the sacred space interrupting any form of reverence that might have been present. Being of ruddy complexion, I blushed furiously and, joining ranks with other fallen angels, plummeted to the floor. Wishing I had the magic to just disappear, I felt just like "The Lone Wild Fowl in Lofty Flight" who wanted to fly the coop to Never Land or Oz.

While I was never found guilty of breaking wind or any other commandment, my boyhood countenance was shattered, and my choral virtue was questioned. Of course, I wanted revenge, but with Christmas just a few days away, my main concern was being a nice Christian and keeping off the naughty list that Santa was purported to be keeping on us around this time of the year. Even fallen cherubs deserve a break!

12/8/2019

# Carols in a Jail

Our children's choir went to sing in the city jail on the Sunday prior to Christmas one year. I remember it so well and can almost picture that large room holding three layers of cells on three walls. We walked in through the jailer's office, down the wooden steps. The place was rather dark and dank with some unpleasant smells beyond my olfactory experience at that time. We stood on the rather wet concrete floor, all dressed in our white robes with red bows. And we were all afraid of the unknown.

The whole place was lighted by a huge single 300-watt bulb suspended in the center of the room of twenty or so cells, barely illuminating the figures that had now risen and were peering down at us through the bars. For reasons that were beyond my knowing at the time, these prisoners were all black men; so their countenance was even more obscured by the darkness, save only the whites of their eyes which seemed to be staring right at me. An eerie silence added to the obscurity of the darkness. This was the most fearful night of my little life so far, and I wondered why in tarnation we had been brought here. I would soon find out.

Someone started us singing "Silent Night, Holy Night". Our little voices were magnified by the cavernous condition of the jail, and we sounded like giants...or at least teenagers! "… sleep in heavenly peace, sleep in heavenly peace"…words ending our first song. A man in the highest level of cells slowly clapped his hands, and a few others soon did the same.

From that first song we somehow mustered our courage to sing "Away in a Manger" and "Hark the Herald Angels Sing". By the end of our repertoire, I almost felt at home in this prison. I felt safe among these men because we had all shared a kind of peace on earth and goodwill toward others that passes understanding. While they might indeed have been a captive audience for our early angelic endeavors of doing good for God's sake, I was captured by the sheer humanity of those prisoners, a feeling that warmed my heart on that cold night and melted the bars between us.

With a gusty round of "We Wish You a Merry Christmas", we ended our first prison concert with gusto. As we started back up the stairs to the freedom outside this forbidding place, the words "Merry Christmas" began ricocheting of the walls, almost as if a heavenly host of angels were shouting down at us. But it was even better than angels; it was our newfound friends...the prisoners in the Canton jail.

As we left, it began to dawn on me why we had come here and the gift that had been given to us by those men behind those bars. We came in scared to death and left with a fuller understanding life. We came in with unspoken prejudices against black prisoners and left with that wonderful feeling of kinship that transcends our conditions of race and creed.

But it was there I also discovered the softer meaning of courage. The kind of courage that stands up in the face of your worst fears, trusting something beyond you to carry you through this moment in spite of your own uncertainty. The kind of courage that would lead me through many a danger and many a fear and shows me how fear can create a prison far worse than the city jail. Once you face your fears with the courage of a simple faith, you move even deeper into wisdom and learn how to live beyond your wildest fears. It was one of those Christmas gifts that is still giving!

12/15/2019

# Madonna and Child

I have problems with the US Post Office this time of year, and it's not just the long lines. It's some of those stamps that make me question the big picture. Fundamentally, I believe in the First Amendment in our country's Constitution which states that "Congress shall make no law respecting an establishment of religion…". The separation of church and state. I happen to be a Christian who lives in this country, but this nation does not -- and should not -- have to give any allegiance to my form of faith. So why put a picture of Mary and the infant Jesus by Bachiacca on a stamp with "U.S.A." and "Forever" imprinted over them?

Furthermore, it seems cheapening to pay that small amount for a miniature print of a masterpiece, suitable for affixing to the envelope of your choice. The artwork itself is antithetical to the biblical themes of Advent and Christmas. Too sterile and surreal. Too clean to be honest; too good to be true to the poverty and homeless condition of the terribly young couple from Nazareth forced by the state to go to Bethlehem to be enrolled. The town was so crowded that there wasn't a place to stay. The barn had to do.

Do you begin to see some of the contradictions at work? The state -- Rome in the First Century -- imposes its religion. The only king is Caesar. Then sets out to shove the Jews from hither to yon, at the state's whim. Rather than being artistically glorified, the

Madonna and Child were victims of inconsiderate and impersonal political convenience. They were helpless immigrants. And homeless aliens. And hopeless, save in their convictions of faith that somehow knew that no matter who ruled the kingdoms, Jehovah God would have the final word. Little did they realize that that word would come in this situation.

That Word did become flesh. Dwelt here with the likes of us, except his was a world of poverty; no place to lay his head until he leaned finally against a Roman cross and was laid to rest in a borrowed tomb.

Our faith always demands that our ultimate loyalty and trust be in our belief that the kingdoms of this world will have their day, but the Kingdom of God is always underground quietly becoming a place of peace and love. No matter where we might live on this globe, or under what flag, we'd best pledge our primary allegiance to the same Jehovah God who managed in the unseemliness of a manger to be born and have an "official holiday" named in honor of the occasion. The God who makes all our days holy and whose rule extends beyond the borders of any nation or empire.

12/22/2019

# A Real Close Call

As the fake snow begins to melt on the original live nativity scene, all is not well in Christendom. The sheep still need tending and the cattle need lowing and the wise men have been forewarned to forget the star and high tail it out of Dodge to dodge Herod's evil plot to slaughter the babies in Bethlehem.

Threatened by the possibility of a political rival, King Herod's rage turns into a tizzy. He becomes an imperial maniac who feels like this whole Christmas drama about another king being born in his domain was coming a bit too close to home. Too close for comfort. And so the executive order to kill the kids in order to eradicate the unknown suspect. He really did not want to keep Christ in Christmas!

Unbeknownst to the newly born Jesus, his parents must do the best they can to protect their brand spanking new boy. Mary and Joseph were unlikely candidates for bearing a child to begin with. Unmarried and unsettled. Much too young and poor. Without too much common sense. Mary's time for delivery could happen anytime, and they strike off to Bethlehem. No reservations for the inn for the holidays, so it's off to the stables. Inexperienced at midwifery — immaculate or otherwise — Joseph had to figure out what to do with the umbilical cord. The infant mortality rate was high enough in that culture under normal conditions, and here's this freshly born child lying in a cattle feeder. Jesus's birth must have been a real close call, even without the madness of King Herod.

Against all those odds and in the perilous poverty of that night, Mary gave birth to a life that from the beginning courted death. That he survived is miracle enough. The claim that this is Emmanuel -- God with us in the middle of it all -- is almost scandalous to our way of life that seeks safety above all. The life of Jesus was antithetical to our fretful ways of protecting our vulnerability. He seemed to live and die as if he were only a heartbeat away from God. Maybe when God gets that close, it's too close for comfort. Or it could be the only kind of comfort that finally matters.

12/29/2019

# Slippery Slope of Sloth

Many of us begin our day with a cup of coffee – thanks be to God and the hands that picked those beans and all the middle folk who got it to the house and the brewing machine. That's the best cup of all. My second all-time favorite is the 23rd cup that shows up at the end of a psalm by the same name and number.

The perpetual problem with this cup of biblical proportions is that it is always spilling and overflowing. The other issue is that the cup owners must put up with all the goodness and mercy that follow them all the days of their lives. And to beat all, you end up living in the house of the Lord forever! How's that going to work? Will the place have enough coffee cups for the early risers? Will stingy cup holders be willing to share their good fortunes better than they ever did in this life? [Think Lazarus and the rich man in Luke 16]

As many of us recently reveled in the New Year, we also reflected on the goodness of the year just gone. We even joined in singing those ancient words of Robert Burns: For auld lang syne, my dear, / for auld lang syne, we'll take a cup of kindness yet,/ for auld lang syne. For all those good times, let's lift our cups full of kindness in a considerate salute to all God's folk.

There's the cup we certainly could use these days. Kindness has been conspicuously absent throughout the world in the past few years, and it would be a refreshing change to have combo cup of kindness overflowing with goodness and mercy. [No Styrofoam please] Far be it from me to delineate the lack of civility and neighborliness with which we are constantly reminded in the daily news. There hardly seems to be any concern for our common good anymore, and nonchalance is having a heyday as if anyone really cared. Global warming and our cold-hearted shenanigans to shut out others are on a collision course as we begin a new decade. And no one seems to give a rip while protecting their own skin and profit. Another name for this awful uncaring and apathetic attitude is one of the seven deadly sins known as sloth.

Some people think that sloth is what you get when you stay in the tub too long, but it's the worst of the seven deadly sins committed by people with good intentions. They mean well, bless their hearts, but they are letting all the kindness leak out of their own coveted cups in their complete disregard for their neighbors. It's about time we take up arms and live out those words in Ephesians: "Be ye kind one to another, tenderhearted…" Kindness doesn't just appear out of the blue but in the random acts we initiate for the good of the whole. And for God's sake, don't play innocent with your "I just don't know what to do!" or worse, "who cares?" That's **sloth** at its lowest level of enigmatic inertia! We all know what to do when you see it: fetch your cup of kindness and let your goodness and mercy go to work!

1/5/2020

# You Are Here

Airports, hospitals and other assorted large buildings usually have a floorplan map conveniently placed at the entrance. And on that map of gates and rooms, there is that red dot at one end of an arrow; at the other end are the words "You are here". In a confusing world, it is comforting to know where you are every now and then.

Those of us who mark the days passed with a big X-mark have the same experience. Behind today's date is a string of days crossed off — finished. The current day stares at you and proclaims "You Are Here". The days that lie ahead are clean on the sheet.

Whether from the perspective of geography or time, there is some security in knowing where you are. In front of the mall directory you know where you stand; the red dot indicates that. Looking at the calendar, you know where you are in the flow of time, that great leveler of humanity. Each of us is rich with space and time.

Most of the time, at least. But when life becomes confusing. When pain tears us apart. When depression puts us on rock bottom. When failure strikes a low blow. A stroke renders us useless. Alzheimer's takes away our memory. When death of a spouse or child comes suddenly. On those occasions, we have this haunting feeling: where in the world am I? What am I doing here? What kind of place is this? Where's the light switch? The gyroscope inside that gives us a sense of balance and perspective goes haywire. We don't even know what day it is. Or year. Time becomes more of an enemy than an ally. Where is that floorplan with the dot on it?

Faith – the kind the Bible keeps pointing to – has a lighthouse effect in those times and places of our lives when we seemed lost. Whether in the wilderness of failure and despair or in the far country away from home. You might want to check out the man in the middle of the Gospel, who seems to know where he is even though he didn't have a place to call his own. Or look through the Book at the stories of the God who seems to keep going the second mile: in the Garden; on the Exodus; in the promised land. The star in the east. The cross on the hill. The empty tomb. Pentecost. Like red dots scattered across history, wherever God's people are: "You are here, and I am with you."

1/12/2020

# From Resume to Obituary

At some point in our lives, we begin developing our résumés, those documented lists of accomplishments and accolades that we deemed noteworthy. Usually, the purpose of these documents is to impress a prospective employer or the board of directors looking someone to take a higher place in the company. The résumé is the opportune way you promote yourself to others.

Somewhere else along life's way, the necessity of résumés, along with life insurance, diminishes. How many of us needed a résumé in order to retire? Maybe that would be a good idea: utilizing our résumés to prove to some AARP committee that we are worthy of retirement and all of the benefits appertaining thereunto, including reasons why we deserve Social Security.

Or supposing when you came to the very end of your life and you needed that résumé to justify your use of life itself, what would you want it to say, for Heaven's sake? Would you list your membership in a church, along with your attendance and giving over the years? Maybe you'd have a section on your best golf score on the Sundays you weren't able to make worship, or the size and number of fish you caught.

Of course, there ought to be a bottom line on which you could list your net worth — that wonderfully illusive figure for which you wrote all those résumés in the earlier days and for which you gave your time, talent and energy to produce. If money is not your thing, perhaps you could write an essay spelling out your major contributions to humankind and other reasons for which you ought to be remembered by family, friends and all acquaintances. A copy of this essay should be filed with your minister to be used at the funeral or memorial service so that family friends and acquaintances may be reminded of your extraordinary qualities. Finally, it's grist for the obituary bearing your name.

Alfred Nobel had an explosive career and an impressive bottom line. He was worth a bundle for his invention of that powerful stuff we know as dynamite. Not wanting to be remembered as the man who invented the explosive that has caused as much harm as good, he took his powerful fortune and set up the Nobel Prize for Peace.

On December 10, 1964, Dr. Martin Luther King, Jr., would rise to that grand podium in Oslo to accept the accolade on behalf of the cause for which he so nobly gave the last full measure of his devotion. Within a few short years, the assassin would find his mark in Memphis that would change King's legacy into the truest obituary we've ever known. When he accepted the honor in Norway, this is part of what he said: *I think Alfred Nobel would know what I mean when I say that I accept this award in the spirit of a curator of some precious heirloom which he holds in trust for its true owners – all those to whom beauty is truth and truth beauty – and in whose eyes the beauty of genuine brotherhood and peace is more precious than diamonds or silver or gold.*

When the dust settles on our graves, and the stones simply tell the dates of our birth and death with only a hyphen representing all our live-long days, our real obituary will be the unwritten legacy we leave by how we lived and loved and honored all people.

1/19/2020

# Bless Your Heart

One of the great phrases of the south is "Bless your heart!" Remember Tennessee Ernie Ford; he was always "blessing your little pea-pickin'heart." Many southern-culture-challenged folks don't quite know what to make of the term. Maybe, some of you youngn's don't quite know what to make of it either. So, it might be a good exercise for us to expand its meaning for all of us.

For example, it can be an expression of affection: "Bwess its widdle heaaart." Although this pronunciation has limited usage, it's appropriate when speaking to babies and grown dogs. "Bless your heart!" spoken directly to another adult is exuberant shorthand for "Thank you, you're so (fill in adjective appropriate to the situation: nice, clever, sweet, thoughtful, smart, etc.)" without having to get specific, which sometimes comes in handy. I've most often heard hearts blessed in this way in response to the delivery of some kind of homemade something. It is not always sincere.

Of course, being Southern, it's perfectly acceptable to go all the way and say, "Bless your heart! Thank you! You're just so nice, clever, sweet, thoughtful, smart, etc." There's simply no reason to use three words when you can think of nine or 10, that is, unless it's hot. In July and August, you might want to just say "thanks" and duck back inside where it's air-conditioned.

Blessing the heart of someone not within earshot allows us to move into a darker realm without giving up our position of piety or superiority. Nearly always, it's said with a "tsk-tsk" and a sad, slow shake of the head. It's pity yes, but sometimes, pity masking "I told you so." Something like this: "Did you hear about Ola Mae?

Bless her heart, she has it rough. That husband of hers ran off with his secretary, not that anybody's surprised."

The thing about "Bless (blank) heart" is that it's a wonderful absolution for what you're about to say next –– sort of a Southern-fried, reverse Catholicism. Rather than, "Lord forgive me for what I said " it's "Lord forgive me for what I'm getting ready to say," and then going ahead and saying it.

It's a way we can gossip about our friends and neighbors and distant relatives without sounding quite so mean. And you and I both know, nobody wants to be thought of as mean. "Well, you know … bless his heart. . . he's written bad checks all over town."

There are other phrases I could use, like "God love her" which leaves unsaid "nobody else could", and "poor thing" and "it's a shame" but I've found I prefer heart-blessing. It's just so versatile. All kinds of people, from sociologists to columnists, have tried to pin down just what makes Southerners talk out of both sides of their mouths; why we speak in code. Know what? Doesn't matter. Blessing hearts, saying "y'all," loving grits and humoring humidity are all part of the rules for getting along down here. Call it manners or chivalry; call it subterfuge; it's what makes us charming to each other and irritating to our Northern–immigrant neighbors. Not a bad mix if you ask me. I mean, after all – bless their hearts – not everybody can be Southern.

1/26/2020

# The Seat of the Pants

Those of us who are caught up in the struggle to live as Christians find ourselves somewhere in the middle of two styles of operations. There are some who claim that real Christians are those who live "by the Book." They take the Bible literally as the Christian's owner's manual that must be thoroughly studied, stringently obeyed and ardently defended in order to guarantee worry-free miles of living. Others like to fly by the seat of their pants, looking occasionally at the Book but enjoying the scenery and trying to figure out instinctively how to play the situations by ear.

Whatever our style or whatever our definition of Christian living might be, we all tend to learn our lessons the hard way: by being confronted by our own human limitations on this journey from birth to death. When I was a senior in high school, a close friend was killed in an automobile accident. A piece of paper was found in his shirt pocket on which was scribbled the following: "Live your life as a Bible; it may be the only one some people ever read." Vulnerable for some noble thought to guide this eighteen-year veteran, I latched onto that idea. I began diligently learning the Book and struggling to live by the Book. I kept wondering why I couldn't quite master this quest.

Many years later, I am beginning to understand the wisdom in Ezra Pound's words in his A.B.C of Reading: "Men do not understand books until they have had a certain amount of life, or at any rate no man understands a deep book, until he has seen and lived at least part of its contents." Thus, trying to live your life like a Bible means being open to all those corruptible changes that keep occurring to each of us and realizing how down-to-earth that stuff in the Bible really is. How close to home. Which is the basis of our understanding the Incarnation, when the Word became flesh and blood. H. Richard Niebuhr says it well in his book, The Meaning of Revelation: "The revelation of God is not a possession but an event, which happens over and over again when we remember the illuminating center of our history. What we can possess is the memory of Jesus Christ, but what happens to us through that memory we cannot possess."

I vividly remember the occasion when I was being examined as a minister for entry into a certain Presbytery. The vote looked like it might be close. One old gentleman stood and said that he could not vote for me because I evidently did not read from the same Bible as did he. Later, I thanked him for the compliment. And I felt relieved from the presumption that I could embody a Book like that.

I'm still out here winging it along this journey and kicking myself in the seat of the pants for doing such a lousy job. Maybe somewhere along the road some Judge will throw the Book at me. That's the risk. Beats being having your head buried in some old book. And the scenery is very nice, especially some of the people you meet along the way. Many is the time I feel like old Jacob confronting Esau with those precious words: "To see your face is like seeing the face of God." What a revelation worth more than the book itself.

2/2/2020

# The Beaten Path

I hold my late father-in-law in high esteem not only for his beautiful first-born daughter, but because he was an avid hiker. After his retirement from a college teaching career, Sam hiked the Appalachian Trail, that ancient foot-beaten corridor that led Native Americans and the early vagabond settlers along the spine of this country's eastern mountain ranges. People are forever walking where some angels feared to tread and others have forged their way through the wilderness.

Robert Frost tempts us to consider the road less travelled, but there just might be some conventional wisdom in staying on the beaten path. Over generations, people have figured out the obvious logic of the shortest distance between two points. Even cows follow the well-worn way to the trough. There is a ring of truth in Emerson's wisdom: "If a person can write a better book, preach a better sermon, or make a better mouse-trap than his neighbor, though he builds his house in the woods the world will make a beaten path to his door."

While there may be a danger in beating a path to nowhere in particular or fooling ourselves into taking the primrose path, there's something in our bones that is intrigued by the traces of human wisdom in a well-worn trail to somewhere. Paths capture our imaginations and lead us to all sorts of interesting places. Remember the Wonderland that Alice discovered in the hole at the end of the path? Or Dorothy's fateful trek along the yellow-brick road to the Emerald City.

The Bible is full of paths. We're all familiar with that path of righteousness in the twenty-third Psalm, but do you remember ancient path of Jeremiah? "Thus says the Lord: Stand at the cross-roads, and look, and ask for the ancient paths, where the good way lies; and walk in it, and find rest for your souls." [Jeremiah 6:16] In the far country of separation, the son of a prodigal father stood at the crossroads of his life and remembered the inviting road toward home. He had used it as an escape; now it would become the route toward redemption — the well-remembered path toward home.

Jesus and his disciples didn't try to hack a new road through the religious landscape. Nor did they try to force everyone down some straight and narrow trail of harsh legalism. Instead, he paved the way for us to use the path of love to restore our lives and reclaim our relationships. The French political revolutionary, Andre Malraux, puts it like this: "The genius of Christianity is to have proclaimed that the path to the deepest mystery is the path of love."

For centuries ever after, people of all walks of life, have followed the beaten paths to the doors of cathedrals and churches throughout the world. They have sat for cumulative hours on pews ripe with patina. They have brought their babies to be baptized, witnessed weddings and cried at funerals. They have sung songs and prayed prayers and endured sermons. And in the wonderful famil-iarity of this well-worn trail, there they discovered with those early disciples that Jesus is indeed the way that finally mattered most.

2/9/2020

# The Christian Thing to Do

In Anthony Trollope's novel written in the early 1860's, entitled <u>Framley Parsonage,</u> there is an intriguing passage which describes the way in which one of the characters of the book forgives another: "Of course, Mrs. Grantly forgave Mrs. Proudie all her offenses, and wished her well, and was at peace with her, in the Christian sense of the word, as with all other women. But under this forbearance and meekness, and perhaps, we may say, wholly unconnected with it, there was certainly a current of antagonistic feeling which, in the ordinary unconsidered language of everyday, men and women do call hatred."

Forgiving yet hating! We all know the contradiction. We felt it when we were children. Our parents made us shake hands and accept our friend's apology, but all the time we were plotting how we would get even. We feel the tension as adults when we try to forget how someone has wronged us. Long after we said, "I forgive you," the sting of our wound persists. We keep rubbing it as though it were a physical scar and recalling how it was inflicted. And each time we touch the sore we conjure up its initial pain. Oh, nobody, but nobody knows how we suffered!

Vengeance has a delectable sweetness, but we pay a terrible price for feasting on its fruit. It clogs love's arteries with self-righteousness and reduces our interpersonal relationships to a legal contest in which we keep track of every wrong.

Forgiveness does not come from moral obligation. It requires something stronger than a sense of duty to break through our bitterness. If we forgive because we <u>ought</u> to, we will be like Mrs. Grantly. The novelist pictures her as a "Christian lady" who is at peace with her opponent "in the Christian sense of the word." Like many believers, Mrs. Grantly transforms the spontaneous, heartfelt character of grace into a formal, rigid legalism.

Of course, Mrs. Grantly forgave Mrs. Proudie. Of course! Because social convention demanded it. Because she knew it was proper and fitting. Because from the time she was a child the Church told her it was what God commanded. Because it was a Christian thing to do.

All of which begs yet another question for next week's sequel: What would Jesus do?

2/16/2020

# What Would Jesus Do?

Though the story seems apocryphal, it carries its own veracity when you have heard it out. It comes out of the soul and psyche of the Southern church in its heyday of racial unrest some half a century back.

Like many of its ilk, a certain genteel congregation in a large Mississippi Delta city was struggling with the issue of admitting "people of color" into their morning worship services. In spite of the signs in front proclaiming "Everybody Welcomed" and hymns intoning, "We are not divided all one body we", this predicament straddled denominational lines throughout the town. Even Presbyterians. Especially Presbyterians!

After months of struggling with the question, the Session did what seemed best: they appointed a committee who deliberated diligently and finally decided. The matter would be handled at a called meeting of the Session following morning worship on a particular Sunday.

The congregational matriarch's oldest son was a very influential member of the community and a voting member of the Session which met that day after church. As tradition demanded, the family waited for the meeting to end before gathering at grandmother's home for Sunday lunch. When the Elder brother came through the front door, his loving mother simply inquired, "Well, what did y'all decide to do about this matter at my church?"

The ice was broken, the chase cut, and the issue brought squarely into the dining room on this day of sabbath rest. "Now, Mother, why don't we enjoy our Sunday dinner before talking about that. You know how much it upsets you!"

"Son, we will not sit down to eat until you have told me what the Session has decided to do with my church."

"Mother, let me ask you what you think Jesus would do in this case?"

"Oh, I know what Jesus would do; he'd say we should let them in. But he'd be wrong!"

2/23/2020

# There Must Be a Mistake

For some people that phrase is a simple declaration; for others it's an imperative with a great big exclamation point at the end! There are people who, for whatever reasons, feel constrained to meander through the maze of daily life looking for the flaws. They read books primarily to find a typographical error or a dangling participle before they can get to the pure enjoyment of reading.

Of course, there are people in our society for whom this critical attitude is part and parcel of their vocation. Umpires are there to call 'em as they see 'em. The state trooper sits on the roadside with a radar detector looking for that person who has a faulty speedometer. Math teachers have red pencils beyond number. There are even some preachers who spend their energies looking for sin [a theological term for a mistake] among their congregants. And don't forget the politicians who spend 98% of their time, energy, and rhetoric in pointing out the mistakes of the other party's candidate or legislative initiative in order to look a little better.

Seems like I'm always running into the radar range of these fault finders and name takers. They have a way of making you feel a bit uneasy as well as unworthy. They are not necessarily mean folk nor do they really intend to harm you. And if they catch you red-handed in some little foible, you'll know what they are thinking. Your attempt at an excuse — "Sorry about that. We all make mistakes" — will fall on ears that don't connect to any part of the heart.

On his way to death row, Jesus was always in the cross hairs of the religious right wingers and like-minded politicians who were out to get him for blasphemy. Another mistake or two, and we've

111

got enough to try him and crucify him like any other criminal. And before Pilate at point blank range he was asked to give up truth itself as any form of defense. To consider Jesus as a manifestation of God's truth would be the biggest mistake of all! Crucify him! And we did.

3/1/2020

# Under the Circumstances

They are all around us. As obvious as the nose on your face. Like the sky above us, we all live "under the circumstances". Why, just in the last few weeks, circumstances seem to be in a tailspin. The coronavirus outbreak, the stock market plunge, the end of our twenty-year war in Afghanistan, and the upcoming elections. Underneath all these obvious changes, the climate keeps changing for the worse, the population keeps expanding and refugees can't find a home.

Speaking of refugees, Jesus lived his life under such circumstances. He knew them and accepted them for what they were worth. They were the givens. The Creed lists a few: "born of the Virgin Mary, suffered under Pontius Pilate; was crucified, dead and buried...." Of course, there were more circumstances in his life than those, but those were enough to send any man to his grave. Which, in fact, is exactly what happened.

So, his story is not too different from ours. The opening verb describes each one of us to the T: "born". That's what you might call the first condition — we all came to life under the circumstances of birth. [There were certain circumstances that led to our conception, but let's not get into that here.] We have all, in some form or fashion, "suffered". If not under Pontius Pilate, we've had to live as political creatures under circumstances that are less than ideal. We've even had things happen to us that seemed at the time like crucifixions of sorts.

And since you are reading this, it means you probably haven't quite experienced the last episode — the final circumstance of death. Those are the basic circumstances of life. The question is: what are we to do about them — these circumstances? Some people would rather deny them. "Under no circumstance" becomes their watchword for never admitting that life has certain limits and bounds. They'd rather be caught dead than declaring that we have to live under circumstances that stifle human capability. Circumstances change, you know. And they do. They can even be changed. But what about birth and suffering and death? Can we change those or can we face them head on?

William Faulkner's <u>Go Down, Moses</u> is a collection of poignant stories that speak mightily to the human condition. In one of the stories, *Delta Autumn,* he writes "There are good men everywhere, at all times. Most men are. Some are just unlucky, because most men are a little better than their circumstances give them a chance to be. And I've known some that even the circumstances couldn't stop."

Prince Hamlet tried to warn us about "the slings and arrows of outrageous fortune...the heart-ache and the thousand natural shocks that flesh is heir to..." During the original lent thing and all the circumstances appertaining thereunto, Jesus set his flesh and blood toward what seemed a bitter end. And all we are supposed to do is limit the liabilities of our existence and give up chocolates for forty days.

3/8/2020

# Food, Water & Ammunition

The current concerns over the pandemic COVID-19 virus along with the consequential economic downturns and shutdowns, have begun to rattle our nerves and undermine our faith and hope in the future. It's been eye-opening to see how human beings begin to hoard stuff at times like this in a frenzy akin to life-boat mentality. Over my limited lifespan, I have encountered several times when the world was expected to come to an end, beginning with the threat of nuclear war in the 1950's when bomb shelters were popular in many backyards and stocked with cans of c-rations.

Most of the traumatic forecasts came from zealot Christians who happen to believe Jesus was coming back to take only the good folk with him to their heavenly reward.

In the 1960's, the Reverend Jerry Falwell of was pushing the sale of his video tape on his TV networks which will give you all the information you need to know about this soon-to-be-horrendous experience for just $29.95. [What he did with the proceeds of these sales after the rapture thing is a mystery to me.] On the tape he suggests to the hard-core believers that they begin to stockpile food, water and ammunition in preparation for the end of the world.

The next tribulation to come along was the impending millennium, leaving behind a few survivors. Most of the naysayers who were pushing this doomsday junk have this basic assumption that the world is such an evil place with such awful people in it. But the day is coming when Jesus will return and put an end to all this misery. And guess who's got a ticket out of here? Only those who have made their resolutions for the coming year not to sin and to put the water bottles and ammo under their beds.

The next big date was in May of 2011, when hard-core Christian Family Radio's Harold Camping convinced his followers that the Bible prophecy led him to this conclusion. After that day, he revised his vision to say that May 21 had been a "spiritual" Judgment Day and that the Rapture would occur on October 21, 2011, together with the destruction of the world. Here's one of my favorite photos from early 2011. A more fearful billboard was spotted recently in nearby Anson County stating: "He's up and He's coming back!" If it's fear that floats your religious boat on these troublesome waters, this is good stuff. But there ought be a better way of being God's folk.

Whether it's the impending pandemic, a nuclear war or the threat of the rapture, we've got enough to say grace over in keeping up with what Jesus might have had in mind for such a time as this. He clearly set the agenda for the time being: feed the hungry, heal the sick, care for the suffering, free the oppressed, preach good news to the poor and disenfranchised. Never mentioned stockpiling food, water and ammunition to protect yourself from those in need.

After having read those left-behind books, I'm about ready for those good people to get out of here so the rest of us can go to work on what matters most to the least of these our neighbors. You do know the name for those left behind? Jesus called them the Church.

3/15/2020

# The Waiting Game

Long before the advent of the corona virus into our lives a few months ago, we found ourselves forever waiting. In the express lane of the grocery store or at long traffic lights. At the doctor's office we learn the meaning of being a "patient". We call the insurance company to ask a simple question, manage to work our way through the maze of call options with their series of numbers to punch only to receive a recording that "all of the available agents are busy with other customers…but don't hang up because your call is important to us. Your call will be answered in the order in which it was received." And you waste yourself in all that time, simply waiting on what seems like a trivial pursuit.

There are other — deeper — forms of waiting. Your teenager is out for the evening and long overdue. You stand at the window, peering into the darkness for some glimmer of oncoming light, some indicator that a car has made it safely through your worst fears and is approaching your driveway. Or the lab tests take longer than expected, and your waiting becomes embedded with pins and needles. With the larger fear and threat of where or when this corona virus hanging over the world will strike, waiting undermines our living.

Faith is a form of the waiting game we have all learned to play. It's the "assurance of things hoped for…" Things anticipated. It's a conviction of the unseen, unknown future that something's coming. Something good. Something new and better and lovelier. And our job is to hang around. To wait with the rest of creation that almost seems to be groaning like a mother in childbirth trying to deliver someone or something that will finally be redemptive. Or as the psalmist put it, our souls wait for the Lord, more than the watchmen for the morning.

Frederick Ohler, in his book of prayer poems entitled <u>Better than Nice and other Conventional Prayers</u>, summarizes our feelings like this: *"We wait like…a wife on a widow's walk…a child on the day before Christmas…a father worrying at the window late at night….a mother ten months pregnant….like hostages….captives…. Babylonian Jews. The more we know….the more we know we don't know….and our overstanding gives way to….mystery….humility…. anticipation….patience….and advent."*

3/22/2020

# Tidying Our Faith

British scientist, Richard Dawkins, and I have always felt that "it was so thoughtful of God to arrange matters so that, wherever you happened to be born, the local religion always turns out to be the true one." It's how Jesus turned out to be Jewish, and that's how I ended up being a Presbyterian in the middle of Mississippi nearly eight decades ago. For good or ill, we have inherited our faith from our families over generations simply by circumstance of our birth. If you were able to climb up each limb of the family tree, you would discover how that faith has been promoted and promulgated over the years. You might also find that over the centuries that your faith has become cluttered with more stuff than might be necessary for the living of these days.

As a former member of the clergy with cluttered religious closets, I would like to come out and confess that I was born again. Not with a personal relationship with Jesus Christ my Lord and Savior...whatever that might mean. But as a convert of the Marie Kondo method of tidying up all the stuff in my life. Beginning with my unused clothing and dirty – dusty – books, I was alive to the spirit of this feisty little woman from Japan.

During this intentional home stay hiatus imposed by the corona virus and using the KonMari Method of "tidying up", let's take this stuff out of our spiritual closets and drawers and book-shelves – even the stuff under our beds and lay it all out on the floor. The test will be to see what still fits, what brings you joy, and what serves the common good. Let's look at what might be only religi-osity full of filigree and fluff. Let's see if we can clear the clichés and explore our limited vocabulary to discover what is honestly faithful to the gospel truth within us.

"When I was a child, I spoke like a child, I thought like a child, I reasoned like a child; when I became an adult, I put an end to childish ways." Remember those wonderful words from St. Paul in one of his letters to the Corinthians. When he became a real man, he claimed that he could see a whole lot more clearly because he put away his childish worldview.

When I was a child, in a somewhat similar fashion, my family and household of faith – the Church – started indoctrinating me by imprinting doctrines and dogmas so that I would "grow up and not depart from it." By six, I had memorized the catechism, knew all the books of the bible and knew – by heart – the Lord's prayer with debts and debtors as well as the 23rd Psalm.

They also subtly taught me how lucky I had been not to have been born a Roman Catholic. Or an Episcopalian. Or a Baptist. I learned more about what we did not have in common with those "other" people, than what we were actually supposed to believe. Presbyterians were the best brand of Christians ever conceived by the Holy Spirit and born of John Calvin's virgin wife in Geneva. It was almost immaculate in how it happened.

Even without my tongue-in-cheek sarcasm, you can see we have our work cut out for us: What in our faith still fits us? What brings joy to us and to the world? What serves the common good?

3/29/2020

# The Hell of Easter

When people ask me what I think about hell, I have a very limited repertoire of images and anecdotes. My best image is to clump a lot of my bad memories about Easter into how that first day in hell would be spent.

It would begin with the proverbial sunrise service in the high school gym [due to rain on the football field] with the junior high band playing "Up from the Grave He Arose!" This would be followed by a men's breakfast in the church kitchen with sordid stories from their worst Easters ever. You would move to the morning circle featuring selected readings from The Greatest Story Ever Told. You would then drive for hours without a bathroom break to attend the nearest meeting of Presbytery, accompanied only by an Elder who would cancel your every vote. That would be the beginning of a day when I would have hell to pay for Easter.

All this seems to fit one version of the Apostles' Creed in which Jesus was "crucified, dead, and buried; he descended into hell. On the third day, he rose again from the dead…" Many congregations omit the hell phrase to keep from using a bad word in church. And it's a phrase not to be found in the Bible per se.

Some of us are confused by the different cosmology with hell below in which to "descend" and heaven above in which to "ascend". Without benefit of Galileo or Copernicus, the biblical stories are full of such ups and downs. Even our Lord's Prayer has heaven up there and earth down here. Others refuse to use the phrase because they don't believe that Jesus had to pay such an atonement, while the "elect" believe Jesus died only for them and their kind.

There's an old legend that emerged in the Middle Ages that pictures Jesus descending into hell to release Adam and Eve from torment. Another writer took the story and made it more radical. Jesus shows up at the gate of hell. Satan meets him in a rage, trying to forbid Jesus entering. Jesus cannot be restrained. He tears open the gate and begins his search. As he probes the darkest and most sinister recesses of torment, he releases everyone he finds, but it is clear that he is in quest of some particular one. He hunts even deeper, ever more strained into the bowels of ultimate treachery. Finally, far back and away from all other prisons, Jesus finds a cage of horrifying isolation. He approaches it, and as he does, Satan cries, "No, not that one! That one is my prize!" Oblivious to Satan's objections, Jesus wrenches open the door of the cage and sets the prisoner free...sets Judas...free.

4/5/2020

# Easter in an Egg

 Easter has a way of bringing out my childhood faith full of eggs and bunnies and family photos after church in that new Easter outfit. Back in those good old days in order to continue to hoodwink you, your parents would buy special eggs made of sugar and filled with the risen Jesus. You must remember them: in one end you could peer into a peephole and see the graveyard and Jesus with a raised hand and the sun glowing behind him. It was such a neat way to bring all of it together: eggs, rabbits and resurrections that would warm the cockles of your childhood heart and make the whole episode believable and edible. Once adults felt sure that you were convinced that Jesus was alive, you could eat the egg!

With Easter surrounded with such delectable delights, I never was haunted by the notion that a dead man rose from the grave. When I was a child, I remember seeing Easter in an egg. When I became an adult, I began to realize that it was difficult to allow that egg to hatch into the gospel truth that on the third day he rose again from the dead. The notion of a resurrection was quite a contrast to "here comes Peter Cotton Tail, hopping down the bunny trail…hippity, hoppity Easter's on its way…"

When I became a teenager, the church started treating me differently and made me memorize all those scriptures and catechisms and taught me truths that must be believed in order to save my very soul from hell. When I became a young man, I went to seminary still trying to figure out how Jesus escaped from that Easter egg of mine. When I became an old codger like the one writing this stuff, I am bewitched, bothered and bewildered by the way the church has either lost the risen Lord or kept him frozen in time like that peep show egg of my childhood. We want to keep Christ in Easter and Christmas simultaneously.

Think about all the ways that we try to keep resurrection from happening so that we can stay in control of Jesus and use his name to command others: arguing endlessly about doctrine and scriptural interpretation while we fail to care for Christ among the least of our sisters and brothers, constricting our imaginings of Christ to images that leave us comfortable and undisturbed. We keep Christ buried by denying his commands to love our enemies and caring for those who don't even think like us. We spend the church's energy wrangling about those who seem unworthy of God's love.

One year, in the church of my childhood, we put Easter in a shoe box. It was a Sunday school project like unto that sugar egg with the resurrection inside. We each brought an empty shoe box, created Jesus cutouts, and used the green stuff in which bunny rabbits used to lay their jellybeans. We recreated the first Easter inside the box with the lid off, then cut a hole in one end of the box through which to peer at the miracle we had reproduced. But there was a problem…when you put on the top, it was all dark inside and you couldn't see a blooming thing, especially not the risen Lord.

4/12/2020

124

# Body Parts

In early January, back before this ubiquitous pandemic, I acquired a new knee to replace the one my mother knitted together for my date of birth back in 1942. All those years and untold miles made parting with the old one a form of sweet sorrow.

However, as they say in some body shops, "parts is parts". I picked up a new hip several years back and a brand-new ankle from Duke. So, it will be hard for me to claim that I'm made up of original equipment. But, hey, who's to say that we need to stay in mint condition, and I dare any one of us to try that. Through many dangers, toils and snares we've already come, and God willing, this old body, along with the new parts, will someday get me home.

In addition to bones and joints, I understand you can get hearts and kidneys. Tummy tucks and face lifts are becoming the rage among the AARP group. Remembering Billie Holiday's haunting song about body and soul, I've started searching for a newer and sturdier soul to go with what's left of this body with which to finish the race set before me so when I do shuttle off this mortal coil, I'll have all the thrust necessary to land on Canaan's shore. Or wherever!

After all the Easter hullabaloo, Jesus finally departed this veil of tears. When the dust settled, he did this daring thing to his followers: he called on them to be his body. [Paul elaborates on the Body of Christ and its various parts in Corinthians.] During the Covid-19 crises, the best thing any Body can do is wash your hands for twenty seconds, don't touch your face, keep six feet apart from others, and stay home. So the Body of Christ finds itself "virtually" worshipping on our computer screens or the drive-by, stay-in-your-car Easter resurrection parade.

Something's missing here because, at its core, worship is a contact sport. Even proper Presbyterians prefer proximity. Remember when we came together on a weekly basis in order to sit by each other, pray with each other, shake hands, share stories, and hug each other for dear life. We actively spoke and listened to the Body language of Church. All the body parts did their thing to make a joyful noise and pass the plate and break the bread and drink the cup and leave with renewed energy. Scoffing at reality at times, one hymn declared "we are not divided, all one body we…", but said so within the Beloved Community. We sang to high heavens, and I believe, in the final analysis, those hymns of ours are the blessed ties that bind us together until we meet again.

That's why I enjoy playing my Mormon Tabernacle Choir records and belting out those great choral works in harmony with them. Tapping out "who from our mothers' arms has blessed us on our way" on my new knee. Quietly listening to the music of the spheres. Remembering the words of the Carpenters when they sang…*I got my troubles and woe but, sure as I know, the Jordan will roll, and I'll get along as long as a song is still in my soul…* That's some soul food for thought during these days of distance dancing, especially to the upbeat tune of *Lord of the Dance*.

4/19/2020

# Midwives, Husbands, Single Parents

E.B. White puts words on the tension we feel everyday: *I arise in the morning, torn between a desire to improve the world and a desire to enjoy the world. This makes it hard to plan the day.* That is clearly the healthy tension in which we all live and move and have our being. Between our obligation to those who gave us these undeserved inheritances and those to whom we shall pass it on in the generations to come. Grandaddy had a useful term to describe the first phase: *Beholden.*

"Beholden" means to be obligated, especially in gratitude. To be indebted to someone. We tend to think of this in negative terms. We cherish our independence. We'd rather not owe anyone anything, or be indebted to someone. But, when rightly understood, there's also a positive side to that term. When we understand that life itself is a gift, and when we grasp the debts of gratitude we owe to all those who created and recreated us — formed and reformed us into who we are becoming — then we know in our bones that we are always beholden. And that's when we live more freely by grace rather than by the illusion of our own merits.

The farmer/poet Wendell Berry puts the paradox in these words: *The past is our definition. We may strive, with good reason, to escape it, or to escape what is bad in it, but we will escape it only by adding something better to it.*

The world and the cosmos and history and future are all good gifts around us. We are part and parcel of all this, and we can never escape. And at the other end of the equation, we actively strive for ways to save the creation from destruction so that another generation of our grandchildren can enjoy the dawn or see a hawk soar or stumble over the stardust. Terry Tempest Williams helps us see the big picture like this: *The eyes of the future are looking back at us and they are praying for us to see beyond our own time. They are kneeling with clasped hands that we might act with restraint, leaving room for the life that is destined to come.*

 Every day is Earth Day for us, and we are merely the middle people. Midwives, mid-husbands [practicing good husbandry] or single parents giving birth to the world that is coming to life among us and within us. So it's hard to plan your day when you can't decide whether to enjoy the world left to us by our ancestors or improve it for the generations yet to be born.

4/26/22020

# Living Our Eternal Lives Already

Remember those billboards with that disturbing question: "Where will you spend eternity?" The object of that question was to scare the living hell out of the beholder and encourage him or her to come to Jesus before you die and it's too late to decide. You have to choose, which puts you in the cat bird's seat; a bad assumption. Another bad assumption is that eternal life can't begin until we get rid of this current living situation by dying. Raising yet another conundrum: is there life before death? A lot of religions use this outdated worldview as part of their theological construct to encourage walking the straight and narrow in order to get your eternal reward in heaven knows where or when.

May I be so bold to suggest that we might just be blind to the notion that all of life is sacred and eternal, from the get-go. Since time immemorial, the Creator has endowed us with the gift of days and years forever and ever. That we are already spending our precious lives smack dab in the middle of eternity. Paul Tillich called it "The Eternal Now."

The romantic poet, William Blake, wants us to see this world through a different lens altogether: *To see a World in a Grain of Sand/ And a Heaven in a Wild Flower/ Hold Infinity in the palm of your hand/ And Eternity in an hour.* By the way, living our eternal lives has nothing to do with pantheism or believing that the divine in all of nature. It's much bigger than Mahalia Jackson unequivocally singing that she believed for every drop of rain that falls a flower grows. The one-drop-one-flower theory is soft science at its finest and bad religion at its worst. Right up there with "he's got the whole world in his hands", assuming a gender for the Creator. Heaven forbid!

Such nature worship tends to be oblivious to the big picture of eternity happening all around us as we live and breathe in this infinitely expanding universe. The Brazilian poet, Paulo Colelho, puts it in a more thoughtful fashion like this and ties it to our larger theme of stumbling over stardust: *We are travelers on a cosmic journey, stardust, swirling and dancing in the eddies and whirlpools of infinity. Life is eternal. We have stopped for a moment to encounter each other, to meet, to love, to share. This is a precious moment. It is a little parenthesis in eternity.*

We may wait from here to eternity to see if it's going to get better in the sweet by and by, or we can wake up every morning and thank our lucky stars that the gift of eternity has already been bestowed on us all without our having to do a blessed thing. Well, at least we could relish every minute of it and enjoy the hell out of it, for heaven's sake!

5/3/2020

# Mama's Will

Mama let me be a lot of things, but three of the most important were these: she let me be one of her children; she let me become a minister; and in her later years she let me have her power of attorney. Had I had that "power" first, we could have resolved a lot of other issues… like what size switch was appropriate for the crime!

When she died eleven springs ago, her family and friends gathered in the Chapel of the Cross near her birthplace, and, as a combination of my three roles, I asked them to think of the place as a board room for a corporate law firm in keeping with my power of attorney. In addition to thanking God almighty for Eloise, we came for a more mundane cause: to see what she bequeathed to us in her last will and testament. Of course, we might be taken by surprise as to how close the mundane and the sacred can come in moments like this when we start talking about our inheritance, since that pretty much covers everything that we think we own and are in the first place.

As for her financial portfolio upon her timely death, there remained hardly enough to pay for the cremation and tombstone. No stocks or bonds; no insurance; no equities. The only real claim she had on any land upon her death was half of a grave in her family's burial plot behind this Chapel; she had given the other half to her first-born son after his untimely death, partially explaining her choice to be cremated in order to make more room on the grounds of her rather limited estate. Even though it was less than twenty square feet in size, that piece of earth runs all the way down into eternity. She and Jimmy are doing a timeshare with their parcel of land that now owns them.

So, what's left of Mama's limited estate to share, since there's evidently nothing left to possess? Mama's will is like her grave plot: it makes up in depth what it lacks in length and width. And like her grave plot now possesses her, we can become possessed by her sweet memories of a woman who epitomized will power. She was a strong-willed woman, especially on some days in my childhood. Life got hard for her several times, but her will to do what was right and to be kind, kept her steadfast and content. Mama's will was always for the common good for everyone she knew. She embodied the term "goodwill".

Mama's will changed the nuance of the word itself into the will to live her life thoughtfully and hopefully, in spite of some circumstances that confronted her. A lover of the great game of Rook, she took the cards from the dealer each day and played her hand to the best of her ability. Mama's will determined that the world would be a better place because she cared about all those people in her daily world. Her will could not be contained by the letter of the law since it was so much lived by the spirit of love.

In her last day or two, Mama's will to live would morph into her will to die as if it were part of the game of cards she kept getting. With thankful relief, she moved through her final days and hours in the gracious hands and hearts of hospice caregivers.

When Mama's will to live and her will to die came together that day, you could almost feel and see the greater will of the Dealer playing itself out at the card table of the moment. While I would never presume to know or want to really know what the will of God might be for us, I can at least hope that God will always love us and hold on to us through thick and thin, in health or in sickness, for richer or poorer, in youth and old age, and especially in our dying day.

5/10/2020

# Time To Be Holy

Some of us feel guilty and inadequate when we simply can't find the time to take the "time to be holy, speak oft with thy Lord..." as one old hymn suggests. My quiet moments of solitude, which, in any given decade, are few and far between, are very seldom intentional ones. They happen in a more serendipity fashion when I'm preoccupied with other things less holy than thine.

The world in which I live and move and have my being doesn't have a pause button. Time is like an ever-rolling stream, and each day brings an ever-loving load of things to do. I've come to love all the moving parts, the motion and the commotion. So for me, every moment becomes a chance to do something, even if it's wrong. Even if it's trivial. There's no way this soul of mine can be still for long. I'm a busy fellow who doesn't have a prayer for finding time for meditative moments. However, maybe in the unstructured noises some of us can discover the Holy in the sheer energy of daily motion. We might discover the stardust beneath us when we finally stumble into some of it accidently.

Or we just might discover holiness in other people, like Martin Buber suggests in his book, I and Thou. Or like Jacob on the day he was reconciled with his brother Esau: "...to see your face is like seeing the face of God..." Or as Victor Hugo put it on the barricades of the French Revolution: "To love another person is to see the face of God."

"Holy Moses" might be a powerful expletive, but it is almost a misnomer. Out there with the bleating sheep, a man with a warrant on his head for murder one. His refuge is his work for his father-in-law. Out there keeping watch over that blasted flock by day and night. Not looking for trouble. Not looking for God either. In fact, trying to become incognito. Then out of his peripheral vision he sees what seems to be God, who is also incognito as a burning asbestos bush. Suddenly for Moses, holy ground is right under his sandals where he is minding his own business. Without taking time to be holy, the Holy One of Israel slipped into his schedule and asked Moses to take off his shoes to better feel the stardust beneath his whole body. Busy as a bee and suddenly the whole world is a beehive of activity that becomes, in the words of the Jesuit poet, "charged with the grandeur of God."

5/17/2020

# Uncles of a Bygone War

They became known as "The Greatest Generation", those men and women who served this nation during the Second World War. Those of us born between 1939 and 1945 were called the "War Babies", and 1942 put me smack dab in the middle of the bunch. I don't remember much about that bygone war itself, except for the rationing coupons for sugar and our Victory

Garden in the backyard. I do recall two of my uncles were in that war, one in the Pacific Theater and one who was involved in the D-Day invasion of Europe.

Uncle Marshall Bennett, one of my mother's eight siblings, served in WWII and in the Korean conflict as well. He was in the infantry in the China, Burma, India Campaigns whose missions were to train the Chinese National Army in its resistance to the Japanese occupation and to keep the roads open for the Allied Forces. He received the Bronze Star for his actions in this part of WWII. In 1952, he was called back in the Army to join the UN command under General Douglas MacArthur in the Korean conflict fighting the Chinese Communist Army which had taken over China from the Chinese Nationalist Government he had helped train a few years earlier.

Uncle Baby Brother [so named because he was the last of the four siblings] served in WWII, where he was part of Operation Overlord, also known as the D-Day invasion. He was one of the airborne Rangers who would parachute behind the enemy lines before the beach assaults began. Once on the ground, he was in a house that was shelled that night. One shell landed with such a force that it threw him out of the house where he suffered a broken back. He was shipped to hospital in England where he spent most of the war in a traction. He liked to say that he went to war 5' 6" tall and came out 5' 8". Later, Uncle Baby Brother would become the honorary chaplain of Rudder's Rangers centered in Texas.

 I vividly remember that Thanksgiving at Mamaw's when the front door mysteriously opened during the turkey-with-all-the-trimmings dinner. In walked Uncle Baby Brother in his U.S. Army uniform, creating a holy commotion of tears and laughter throughout the house. No one knew he was coming home that day; coming home with his war wounds and gifts; coming home to see his parents, brothers, sister and nephews. I remember the small package parachute that I threw into the air and watched it descend with an amazing grace to the earth, maybe in a similar fashion to his descent that dark June night in 1944. The gift he brought to Mamaw and Daddy Dave was a matching set of sculpted brass shell casings which sat on the living room mantle for the rest of their lives. The real gift, however, was the unintended guest of honor who was so glad to be home in the best sense of that word, and the ruckus he created that day would rattle the dishes in the China cabinet clear down to this Memorial Day.

NOTE: During this Memorial Day weekend that takes place shortly after the 75th Anniversary of VE Day ending the Second World War in Europe, it seemed appropriate to recall those recent soldiers from my own family experiences who served their country in this heroic endeavor. Might be a fitting memorial for you to find those folk in your own family trees and uncover their military histories before they become part of your own bygone history.

5/24/2020

# How's Your Hyphen?

Had I ever become the prize-winning writer God intended me to be, my first book would have been called *Jesus Never Went to Junior High*, because he didn't give us a clue about dealing with this unique subset of early teenagerism. At some point, however, through something akin to a God-given epiphany and thanks to my pastoral duty of preparing middle schoolers to become church members, I discovered that these really were the "wonder years" as portrayed by a 1980's sitcom. My wife's calling to be a gifted middle school teacher might have had some influence on this opinion.

While teaching many classes of this exciting, bewildering and questionable endeavor over the decades, I figured out that sixth graders were the best suspects because they were still beguilable, gullible and remarkable. Their minds still curious, and their attitudes congenial, both of which would change dramatically in a few months. I chose the spring as the season because after-school root beer floats are at their finest in that time of the year. And since the first lesson involved a field trip to the local graveyard, the weather was more favorable.

Twelve-year-olds freakout because they've never been privy to reading tombstones. They wander around for a bit — awkward and giggling — until I gather them to sit on top of a large flat tombstone at ground level. This is the Presbyterian prelude for that come-to-Jesus-before-Jesus-comes-to-you moment. And this is where the hyphen leaps up and declares to unsuspecting and untainted teenagers that life is limited between the date-of-birth and the date-of-death. Even though it may be cut in stone, you don't take your life — that hyphen — for granite. It's all you get…one hyphen each. Suddenly, God bless 'em, they get it!

Which leads to the bigger questions of the course: what will you do with your hyphen and how in the world does your faith [or lack of it] in God figure into that equation? My job was not to give them pat or slick text-book answers, but to enable them to solve their own problems. My hope in that cemetery was to haunt them into living with their questions for the rest of their hyphenated lives.

On the last day of the last class of my last year before retirement, I gathered my little flock of 10 sixth-grade girls in the church van and sensed that all was not well in Christendom. In their catty way, they were nitpicking each other with minor verbal skirmishing. Prematurely, they were beginning to turn into sour seventh-graders-to-be.

At the end of my own rope and realizing that this was all heading south in a hurry, I called a friend and fellow pastor who raised goats for Heifer International and asked if the new kids had been born. We skipped the root beer floats and headed for the goat farm where there were enough new kids for each irritable communicant to hold one. Miraculously, the bickering yielded to smiling and laughing and civilized behavior all around. After getting them to circle up with their new-born goats, I ended the course with one last question: What does this have to do with being a member of the Church?

Rather than mess up the answer, I turned to my friend and compatriot, "Reverend Currie, what does this have to do with church?" He simply told us all about Jesus' concern for the poor people of the earth, and these goats were predestined to be given to them through Heifer International. Standing there in a stinking circle of goat manure, the class graduated into happy disciples of the kingdom in our midst. God bless 'em!

5/31/2020

# If Tomorrow Never Comes

In his classic love song, "If Tomorrow Never Comes", Garth Brooks knows how to cut to the chase in his music to help us see some of the most important stardust on which we tread daily. In an uncanny fashion, his song poses the same conundrum as the scary childhood prayer some of us dared utter before bedtime: "If I should die before I wake…"

The song and the prayer remind us of the tenious nature our life's timeline and imply a goodness in the past that will stand us good in the unknown tomorrow that might never come. That our portion in life thus far has been pretty darn good with more than enough blessing for one life to hold, like a cup running over with goodness and mercy. Inherent in all of this is the notion that we ought be grateful for every inch of life and especially acknowledge that this just might be as good as it gets should it suddenly come to an end.

Folksinger Susan Werner puts the poignancy and pathos of all this together in her song "May I Suggest", which is the essence of gratefulness for every moment and morsel of life: *May I suggest this is the best part of your life/ May I suggest this time is blessed for you/ this time is blessed and shinning almost blinding bright… There is a world that's been addressed to you, intended only for your eyes/ A secret world like a treasure chest to you/ Of private scenes and brilliant dreams that mesmerise/ A lover's trusting smile/ A tiny baby's hands/ The million stars that fill the turning sky at night/ Oh, I suggest this is the best part of your life.*

Out here in what seems like a God-forsaken time of Covid deaths and rampant racism [one requiring we wear masks while the other requests that we take our masks off], the very idea that this is the best part of our lives seems more like the comedy of the absurd. "Change and decay in all around I see", and the daily news is dismally not worth watching anymore. We can either hunker down in paralyzing and irrational fear for the future or join the battle to change status quo. Werner adds a caveat of social responsibility based on our accumulated heritage from generations past: *There is a hope/ That's been expressed in you/ The hope of seven generations, maybe more/ And this is the faith/ That they invest in you/ It's that you'll do one better than was done before...*

May I join Susan and suggest to you and all of us that above and beneath all of these pandemics is a Providence beseeching us to do justice and love mercy beyond our prowess to prevail. At the end of the day, as they say and as she sings...*There is a song/ Comes from the west to you...comes from the slowly setting sun/ With a request of you/ To see how very short the endless days will run/ And when they're gone/ And when the dark descends/ Oh we'd give anything for one more hour of light/ And I suggest this is the best part of your life.*

SUGGESTION: why don't you just take five, find a big screen and good speakers or earbuds and listen to Susan sing "May I Suggest"

https://www.youtube.com/watch?v=eW1DDSQnEYo

6/7/2020

# At the Mercy of Each Other

This pandemic and the world-wide demonstrations for racial justice dramatically illustrate just how we are so precariously at the mercy of each other. This mercy not only operates close to home but far and wide, like a world-wide web. What happened on a curb in Minneapolis put protestors in the streets of London. How we operate within our personal sphere will have a significant influence on what happens elsewhere beyond our imagining. Keeping our distance and wearing a mask not only protects you from the virus but protects those around you from any contagion you may have. All of this combines to keep the common curve coming down.

Having been through over three months of semi-confinement which seemed like some sort of house arrest, the natives are beginning to get restless for "freedom", even if it might cost the lives of others. Some politicos and others pushing for reopening everything honestly believe that the Dow takes precedence over the deaths. Pro-life Christians want to resume corporate worship in their sanctuary even if might lead to the death of innocent and vulnerable people. Lord, have mercy on such a weird guise of religious freedom.

Nelson Mandella once said that "none of us are free until all of us are free." Someone else once noted that if one person dies of hunger, it's a tragedy. If millions die, that is only a statistic. Clearly, we are at the mercy of each other. Even beyond this particular situation, we are always at each others' mercy. When it comes to taking care of this ever-warming planet, we are so dependent on everyone's consideration and compassion and respect for nature. Wendell Berry says it beautifully in these words: *We have lived by the assumption that what was good for us would be good for the world. We have been wrong. We must change our lives, so that it will be possible to live by the contrary assumption that what is good for the world will be good for us...*

If you think about how greed and consumption have motivated our life styles, it's no wonder that the complexity of reopening the economy at the expense of the death of others begs the question of how faith has gotten lost. Mercy is founded on respectful caring and consideration for others, which is founded on the Golden Rule, which is founded on what Jesus called the best commandments of all of them: love God and your neighbor. To paraphrase a previous notion: none of us are neighbors until all of us are neighbors.

What a wonderful world that would be, where goodness and mercy were not just following us all the days of our lives but leading us into the temptation to take care of each other. Luring us to love one another, for the sake of God who believes in us to do right by each other. Begging us in the prophet's words "to act justly, to love mercy, and to walk humbly with your God".

Shakespeare's Portia speaks to Shylock, the merchant of Venice, about the easy and almost natural way mercy works within and between us if we'd let it: *The quality of mercy is not strained./ It droppeth as the gentle rain from heaven/ Upon the place beneath. It is twice blessed:/ It blesseth him that gives and him that takes.*

6/14/2020

# Legacy of a Lie

Born in India, Rudyard Kipling epitomized the pomp and circumstance of England's global imperialism. Some of his memorable writings include The Jungle Book, Gunga Din, and his powerful poem If: *If you can keep your head when all about you/ Are losing theirs and blaming it on you,/ If you can trust yourself when all men doubt you.../ Or being lied about, don't deal in lies/ Or being hated don't give way to hating...*

Rudyard was also a vital part of the "military-industrial complex" of his day before Eisenhower coined that warning for us all. The Boer War was pivotal in his desire to keep the British Empire dominating that situation at all costs. His world view was tainted with white supremacy, especially as portrayed in his work The White Man's Burden where he urges the United States to take up the "burden" of empire in their dealings with the Philippine Islands and assume colonial control of the Filipino people.

Because of his infatuation with imperialism and war, the English government asked him to write pro-WWI propaganda, an offer he couldn't refuse. Much to his delight his son John attempted to join the Royal Navy, but was rejected on medical grounds due to his terrible eye-sight. He was turned down by the military for the same reason. Finally, he was accepted into the Irish Guards, but only because his father lied about his medical issue and pulled some strings to get him in. Sadly, John died in battle, and sources say he was last seen stumbling in the mud in search of his glasses, which had fallen off during attack.

With or without glasses, it doesn't take too much insight or hindsight to understand how that principle has applied to so many of the wars throughout history. Just the wars in this country's relatively short lifespan were based on misconceptions of truth. For example, some historians speak of America's two original sins: the conquest of those natives already living here before the coming of the pale faces, some of whom sincerely thought that it was their God-given "manifest destiny" to take the land away from those first Americans. And the whole notion that white folk could own black slaves would lead to the irreconcilable conflict of the Civil War. Our ancestors fought tooth and nail over what turned out to be a whole lot more than little white lies fabricated by their fathers. In Dixieland where I was born, many still believe that we were never those terrorists fighting against these United States and that the South won the war of northern aggression.

Thanks to religions, lies can leave their legends in realms other than wars, even when we should know better. Like the flat earth society is still convinced that Copernicus and Galileo were lying about their new-fangled constructs of the solar-centered universe. Bible-thumpers still lay claim to the notion that the world was created in a week about five thousand years ago. The awful scourge of racism is based on a formidable lack of knowledge and its consequential lie which claims that some people are created more equal than others.

Sir Walter Scott coined the phrase "O, what a tangled web we weave when first we practice to deceive." We all know the truth of that in our bones, but nobody felt that more than Rudyard Kipling when he got the word about the death of his son John. That confrontation with such a god-awful truth led him to confess this epitaph to war: *If any question why we died, / Tell them, because our fathers lied!*

6/21/2020

# The Miracle of Movement

This pandemic's stay in place imperative or suggestion is beginning to wear thin with me and others that I know. We are hard-pressed to even get out of the house to run the shortest of errands. We are currently getting three weeks to a gallon of gas. This travel quarantine is not just local but national and global. We've had to cancel at least a couple of bucket-list trips abroad that were previously planned. Travelling is one of our passions, and this thing is stifling our human need for galavanting from hither to thither and beyond.

When I was a small boy helping inhabit that little town in Mississippi, I seldom left the county. I don't remember when, but at some point, I began to sneak off to foreign places and became a closet traveler without the knowledge of family and friends. I journeyed to many places with Gulliver and was fascinated by the lands of Lilliput and Brobdingnag. Alice took me to her Wonderland. David Copperfield welcomed me to England. Tom Sawyer stowed me on his raft trip. And on Saturdays, for the cost of a quarter, I would end up in the South Pacific with John Wayne or in the heart of Africa with Tarzan. Those "far away places" in the gazetteer of one's youthful imagination seemed magical and as alluring as Homer's Calypso was to Odysseus.

Over the years, different kinds of realities crept into my world. Geography taught me location and distances. History showed me stories of territorial conquests. Vocation put me on planes and in cars to carry me up and down the eastern seaboard, and vacations let me see many of the places that had hammered their nails of influence into the framework of my being. New wars led to our learning the changing atlas all over again.

During the past three decades, Peggy and I have led thirty-two tours abroad with friends and neighbors from this part of the world. We started all this globe-trotting as a way of creating community among all the strangers from far away places who were moving into our town and church. Travel beyond your own little world brings you together as you share the larger worlds of different countries and cultures. As a bonus, Mark Twain said: "Travel is fatal to prejudice, bigotry, and narrow-mindedness, and many of our people need it sorely on these accounts. Broad, wholesome, charitable views of people and things cannot be acquired by vegetating in one little corner of the earth all one's lifetime."

Twain's take on this human predicament happened to me over and over in those "faraway places with strange sounding names". My camera and I were fascinated by the lovely faces of all those people passing by in such a small and wonderful world after all. **On the back cover of this book** are a few of my photogenic compatriots from all over this precious planet who only ask that we take the time to just look at each other and notice the family resemblances. This collage is the only snapshot I've ever taken of the God in whose image we all happen to be created. It is also another way of expressing the words of Jacob to his brother Esau: *To see your face is like seeing the face of God.*

6/28/2020

# The Limitation of Statues

Standing nearly 100 feet tall and with a wingspan of over 90 feet, the statue of Christ the Redeemer overwhelms the skyline of Rio de Janeiro, Brazil. From the shores of Ipanema to the football stadiums that dot the landscape, Jesus is both protector of the beach beauties and mascot for the soccer teams. Such a huge concrete example of the redeemer should never be taken for granite. Given its defensive position on top of one of the city's highest mountains, this is one magnificent monument that will resist being toppled any time soon, lest it fall on its assailants. Putting Jesus on such a pedestal runs counter to almost everything he taught us about living with each other. However, many a missionary would beg to differ because their motto and mission was to conquer the world for the Church and/or whatever empire might be landing on these shores to enslave the natives, for Christ's sake.

Another formidable figure is the Statue of Liberty, a gift from the people of France, which was dedicated in 1886. Two important symbols capture her message. A broken chain and shackles lie at her feet as she walks forward, commemorating the recent abolition of slavery. After its dedication, the statue became an icon of freedom lifting her lamp beside the golden door and welcoming immigrants arriving by sea, those "huddled masses yearning to breathe..." This certainly was appropriate at this time when most of our population was composed of immigrants from so many different nations. If her beauty lies in the eyes of her beholders, she'd bring tears to freshly freed slaves and new immigrants seeking their liberty and pursuit of happiness on these welcoming shores. This is who we are as a nation, then and now.

 In the beholding eyes of a preschool boy in Richmond, Virginia, the venerable vestige of Robert E. Lee on Monument Avenue was different from that of his father's. Their Sunday morning ritual for a long time was to have breakfast at a nearby restaurant and walk over to see the monument of Lee astride his faithful horse, Traveller. The time came for them to move from the former Capital of the Confederacy, so they went to behold the monument for the last time. As they were walking back home, the child asked his father a very poignant question: "Dad, we've come here every Sunday morning to pay tribute to this famous hero, but you have never told me who that was riding Robert E. Lee." By the way, Lee was not a fan of statues honoring Civil War generals, fearing they might, in his words, "keep open the sores of war."

Perhaps the most complicated predicament is in Arkansas which finds itself between a rock and a hard place with the law of the land and the law of God. You've heard about the Ten Commandments Statue on the grounds of the state Capitol. Several years back, they arrested a fellow for pushing the first granite monument to the ground and breaking all the commandments in one fell swoop. The newly minted stone engraved in the original King James English [another idol of sorts] is being challenged in court this month. On one hand, the Constitution forbids a religious statue on state property, and God's law says you shouldn't have graven images anyway [commandment #2]. Surely, some slick politicians can figure out how to bear just enough false witness [commandment #8] to get this problem solved once and for all without losing their heads like Denis, patron saint of Paris. Bless his heart!

7/5/2020

# Heavens Above!

Starry, starry nights in early winter can take your breath away and open your eyes to one of Mother Natures' silent spectacles. Pitch black dark and a sky dazzling with multitudes of twinkling stars. My mission was to combine oratorical skills with astronomical knowledge to convince the church's youth group that we may or may not be all alone in the universe, but we can certainly enjoy and appreciate it, for heaven's sake.

The group of teenagers and chaperones drove to one of the remote pastures within a few miles of the church and far away from any lights. Each one brought a sleeping bag and willing attitude to expand their horizons. They distanced themselves on the grass as the final aspects of dusk yielded to the enveloping darkness of a moonless sky. The stage was set; the curtain ready to rise shortly. The only thing lacking was a more contemplative audience!

Here's where a form of yoga works its magic in relaxing the mind of the young and the restless. I ask each of them to find a star, any star, and fix their gaze on it. Then draw an imaginary line from their mind to that star so that they might put their minds on those lines and travel to and fro between the pasture and that point in space. After this experience has settled them to a more focused way of seeing things, they are then asked to relax, close their eyes totally, while breathing deeply. Relaxing. Eyes closed. After counting from ten to nothing, I ask them to open their eyes. I wait for the corporate gasp as they experience the pristine glory of the cosmos right above their bodies. In the bleakest of blackness, stars show off their brightest and best.

"Please hold on for dear life," I warn them, "because you are now travelling nearly 70,000 miles per hour as the earth rotates on its axis and makes its way around the annual solar orbit." This does not include our galactic speed through the rest of the universe.

Now the stage is set for a conversation about the canopy of stars in the heavens above. The stories include how some cultures developed constellations and accompanying stories for nightly sightseeing and storytelling. It's a great chance to talk about how the creation might have been formed with a big bang 13.8 billion years ago or a super god who whipped it up within a week about five thousand years ago.

After exhausting all the possible questions about the universe for which few answers were readily available, it was time to wrap up the evening with that question of all questions. Using my best bravado and ministerial machismo, I yelled into the vault of sky above "Is there anybody out there?" After the question ricocheted off the pine trees and a pregnant pause calmed what breeze was out there, a small miracle happened: a huge shooting star crossed the night sky in simple and silent splendor. Without daring to add any of my hubris to such an astronomical epiphany, we quietly exited the grassy amphitheater of our shared sense of wonder.

7/12/2020

# Skyrockets

Was it only fifty-one years ago today when those astronauts walked on the moon? Seems like light year ago when the whole world waited with bated breath to see this culmination of all our endeavors in space beginning with the Sputnik in 1957. The intervening years of space exploration have had their ups and downs.

The most tragic moment for us earthbound observers was that explosion of the Challenger right after its launch in 1986, ending the lives of all seven of the crew members and putting a halt to any future launch for over three years. Not only did it force us to rethink our rocket science, but the failure also to launch raised larger questions about our space programs altogether.

What haunts me to this day about this tragic incident seems like some uncanny cosmic coincident. When all of this went down, I had been reading a book of daily devotions entitled <u>Through the Year with Thomas Merton</u>. Merton was a Trappist monk and mystic for whom I had great admiration. The entry for the day following the Challenger tragedy, was about mental prayer.

*Mental prayer is therefore something like a skyrocket. Kindled by spark of divine love, the soul streaks heavenward in an act of intelligence as clear and direct as the rocket's trail of fire. Grace has released all the deepest energies of our spirit and assists us to climb to new and unsuspected heights. Nevertheless, our own faculties soon reach their limit. The intelligence can climb no higher into the sky. There is a point where the mind bows down its fiery trajectory as if to acknowledge its limitations and proclaim the infinite supremacy of the unattainable God.*

*But it is here that our "meditation" reaches its climax. Love again takes the initiative and the rocket "explodes" in a burst of sacrificial praise. Thus, love flings out a hundred burning stars, acts of all kinds, expressing everything that is best in humanity's spirit, and the soul spends itself in drifting fires that glorify the Name of God while they fall earthward and die away in the night wind.*

Not only did that reading for that day send shivers down my spine, it hit some nerve that went clear to my heart and soul. While it was just a coincident, these different experiences coalesced into a sum that was much greater than the parts, creating a kind of spiritual synergy. Merton had died in 1968, and this collection of his works had just been published in the fall of 1985, five months before the rocket's dreadful demise. Mysterious would-be understatement.

How can we ever forget where we were when that first rocket left the launch pad or when that astronaut took that step and leap for us all on the lunar surface just fifty-one years ago? We were mesmerized by those magic moments on a small screen in our living rooms and dens as we all virtually lifted off toward the stars "expressing everything that is best in humanity's spirit."

*7/19/2020*

# Who Owns the Sun?

To date, no one owns the sun or the moon or the planets. Not even a simple star! You can "wish upon a star". You can "catch a falling star and put it in your pocket". You can "hitch your wagon" to one. You can whistle along while Willie Nelson sings about that "stardust melody". Don't think about owning the temporary Comet Neowise that's been skirting our evening skies recently!

Some people have been snookered into buying stars for their loved ones or friends, and that's how my name has become attached to half a star in the constellation of Aquarius, as in "this is the dawning of the age of...". According to an official gift certificate presented to me and my wife by a friend through the International Star Registry, which lists the telescopic coordinates of our astronomical namesake, I really do have connections with the heavens above. Said Star Registry claims "there is no greater honor than writing one's name among the stars." Just overnight, I became half a star with my better half laying claim to the same great honor.

Let me make it clear, especially to the property tax folk, that there is no legal claim that we actually "own" this star at all. The company that hoodwinked the folks to purchase the aforementioned star in Aquarius, is a very earthbound entity. So, let's get down to earth on the matter of ownership. For it's there — down on earth — that we humans have laid claim to every parcel of property and every acre of land we can find. Staked it out in metes and bounds and put our names on it. Mark Twain once noted that

"Man is the only patriot. Sets himself within the lines of his own country and hires assassins at a great price to protect those lines. We have done this so that there is not an acre of earth left that is in the rightful possession of its owner."

When all's said and done, this earth of "ours" is merely another heavenly body which we have parceled into time-sharing nations and states and street addresses on which we may live from generation to generation. When you take a snapshot of it from the edges of our universe, it looks like every other star in all of those constellations that fill the nightly skies. Just a "pale blue dot", as Carl Sagan once dubbed it. Maybe someone on a far distant galaxy has been bamboozled into buying this thing for which there "is no greater honor than writing one's name among the stars."

What if we owned up to the fact that we are all just visiting travelers on this immense journey through space and time. We can walk out of some starry night, look up and connect those points of light with lines of our own to create our personal constellation akin to Aquarius or the Gemini twins or even the Little Dipper whose handle ends with Polaris by which others might determine true north and navigate their way of seeing through the foolishness of owning any star to begin with, even for just one brief shining moment.

7/26/2020

# Heretics & Heroes

Way back in history, those precious people would think some of the most unthinkable thoughts and do the most outlandish things to earn that combo category of heretic and hero. My early heretical heroes were Job, Jesus and Joan.

Job was considered outside the pale of faith by his three pietistic friends who tried to convince and convict him that his past sins had lead him to the god-awful predicaments of what was left of his miserable life. They were in effect trying to tell Job to "get right with God" or "come to Jesus", except there was no Jesus yet.

When Jesus finally arrived, even in such a miraculous fashion, it didn't take too long for the religiously right people to label him and his heretical ways so off the chart to eventually lead to his death as a punishment by the state for his outlandish thoughts and deeds; like healing the sick people... on the Sabbath...for God's sake!

In the fifteenth century Joan of Arc pushed the envelope in her victorious quest to lead a French army to rescue Orleans from the English during the Hundreds Year War. She was caught and turned over to the English forces who convicted her of witchcraft, relapsed heresy [a capital offense],and cross-dressing, which was also considered a form of heresy. She was burned at the stake in 1431, and according to holy rumors, St. Peter greeted her at the pearly gates with the exclamation "well done!" She was posthumously acquitted, and the Roman Catholic Church made her a saint in 1920.

Galileo Galilei came along about a century after the bonfire of Saint Joan. You know the story...the moons of Jupiter led him to ultimately surmise that the earth was not the center of anything in particular. The Church of the Almighty Answers, of course could not abide such a thing. During Galileo's trial, Cardinal Bellarmine put it like this: "To assert that the earth revolves around the sun is as erroneous as to claim that Jesus was not borne of a virgin." Galileo remained under house arrest until his death. Three hundred and fifty years later, in 1992, the Pope acknowledged that the Church had erred in condemning Galileo for asserting that the Earth revolves around the Sun.

The late congressman John Lewis was one hell of a hero in my book. I was enthralled by his honest courage to fight against the odds to make this nation live up to its founding credo. He got into a lot of "good trouble" in his day and came near death several times. He and his cohorts were taunted targets of every sort of hate and called by every name under the sun, like "anarchists", "agitators" and "godless communists". For all practical purposes, they were heretics

Yet Lewis and his kind came as close to living out the Gospel Truth than many of the Christians who were casting all sorts of aspersions on black lives and trying to keep them from mattering. Trying to prevent them from voting or attending white folks' worship. On that road out of Selma, they were marching to Zion as much as they were heading toward Montgomery. While considered *persona non grata* in his earlier days, John Lewis put his flesh and blood — his heart and soul — on the line, again and again, to bring the sacred words of "America the Beautiful" to full fruition: **"O beautiful for heroes proved/ In liberating strife, / Who more than self their country love/ And mercy more than life."**

8/2/2020

# What Happened to Status Quo?

Memory lane is lovely, meandering through the recollections of how much better life was in the good old days full of traditional values when men were men and women were just women! And if black lives did matter then, they didn't have too much to show for it since they were not allowed to vote. And don't forget those water fountains and segregated toilets. Those were also the good old days when northerners lived in the north before we ever had air-conditioning. As the country music sings it: "Nostalgia ain't what it used to be!"

In the church of my childhood in the fifties, there was a hierarchy of characters, including my grandfather and uncle, who were called Elders who did their duty in a very seemly manner. They were the ones who took the white cover off the silver communion set and folded that linen cloth as if it were an American flag. [Later, I discovered that the theological reason for the covering was to keep away the flys.] These Elders were all men, all white, and all old. And like the uncovering of those sacred sacraments of light bread squares and grape juice, they were the epitome of *status quo*.

If you were a WASP, you had status and had your way in running city hall as well as the local school. In a parish in Mississippi, only protestant preachers could properly pray over high school football games, preferably the long-winded Baptists who proverbially ended everything "in the name of Jesus Christ, our Lord and Savior". The principal called to ask if I would pray under the Friday night lights, and I told him I'd like to invite my good friend the rabbi to come in my stead. I was taken off the prayer list!

Maintaining *status quo* has been a mantra for many civilizations and organizations throughout our past. When I was growing up, we were taught that you just don't mess with things that are *status quo*, even if you felt uneasy about "our way of life" in those old days where "Old times there are not forgotten." That haunting phrase from the song "Dixie" formed the crypt in which we quietly stashed our racism and religious preferences and national resentments toward those patriots of the union who actually won that war we called the "recent unpleasantness".

In the early part of this year, unexpected calamities turned our *status quo* upside down and inside out and spilled it all over creation. Nothing seems the same as it was before the virus crept into our bloodstreams to remind us of the extremely fragile nature of our existence and how we are all part and parcel of each other's wellbeing. George Floyd's helpless and senseless death right there in front of us all opened up another can of worms just waiting on that larger truth that is still marching on in spite of us. *Status quo* has gone with the wind.

At the end of June, the legislature of Mississippi removed the Confederate battle emblem from the state flag, a seismic shift of the needle in recognizing that such *status quo* needed to be changed for the greater good. In a little over a fortnight Georgia's Congressman John Lewis died and left this holy hope for all of us to read the next day: "When historians pick up their pens to write the story of the 21st century, let them say that it was your generation who laid down the heavy burdens of hate at last and that peace finally triumphed over violence, aggression and war."

8/9/2020

# Holy Assumptions

Did you hear the one about the priest who died and went to heaven, a holy assumption to begin with. When he got there, Peter welcomed him and told him that because of his sterling record on earth he would be granted any wish in heaven. Without hesitation, the priest said he'd like to have an audience with the Virgin Mary. In short order, even by heavenly standards, he was sitting in a lovely Victorian drawing room with the Virgin herself. She asked what she could do for this almost perfect priest who went straight to the point: "On earth we adored you and venerated you. Every sanctuary had statues and portraits of you. However, I kept noticing how depressed you seemed…how your countenance was always forlorn. Why was that so?"

"Can you keep a secret?" Mary responded.

"Of course," he replied, "I'm a priest!"

After making sure they were alone, Mary leaned over, tilted her nimbus, grabbed her rosary and whispered in his good ear: "I always wanted a girl."

The high and holy Feast Day of Mary's Assumption happens annually on, or about, August 15.

In other words, yesterday. You may assume that Presbyterians had no earthly idea about it. When I was growing up, we did not know what Advent or Lent were, since they were Catholic, and we weren't. My only childhood association with my neighbor, Father McCarthy, was that he let me keep his Cocker Spaniel when he went back to Ireland in the summer. And Uncle William slipped me into the back balcony for Mass with him when he would sing

"Ave Maria." Let me also dispel the notion that this holy day had anything to do with the opening joke about Mary's little secret, assumed or otherwise.

The Assumption of the Blessed Virgin was hearsay for centuries. Heavenly innuendo derived from the divine and immaculate obstetrics of that first Christmas, and the fact that Jesus lived at home for so long. But in 1950, the Pope sealed the deal. After consultation with the other guys — Bishops and Cardinals in their fancy getups — he defined the Assumption of Mary to be a dogma of faith: "We pronounce, declare and define it to be a divinely revealed dogma that the immaculate Mother of God, the ever-Virgin Mary, having completed the course of her earthly life, was assumed body and soul to heavenly glory." The Wikipedia rationale: "…since Mary is closely associated with all the mysteries of Jesus' life, it is not surprising that the Holy Spirit has led the Church to believe in Mary's share in his glorification. So close was she to Jesus on earth, she must be with him body and soul in heaven."

A few innocent conjectures seem necessary. Joseph was not part of the assumption deal because he was assumed to be innocent of the original conception. One theory is that he got a job in purgatory running a home for unwed fathers. Of course, I believe there's a more practical reason to assume Mary's Assumption into heaven: she needed to be there for the interview with the priest in this morning's first paragraph.

8/16/2020

# Finding Humor in the Holy

I seem to have been born with more than one funny bone, and humor has always been a vital part of my life. If, as the hymn suggests, "prayer is the soul's sincere desire", a good laugh is the soul's sigh of relief for being human. And if we can develop this capacity to smile at the absurdity of ourselves, first of all, and then at all that's going on around us, we just might have tapped into one of the deepest wells of faith with the realization that humor was one of the best ways we experience God and put up with each other.

For example, some Christians I have known are deadly serious about the whole religion business, and some of their antics are no laughing matter. They will fight — tooth and nail — with anyone who dares crack a smile at their righteousness or their God-given notion that they are heaven-sent and heaven-bound creatures whose primary work on earth is to condemn the worthless others whose lives don't matter anyway. These overly sincere Christians, bless their hearts, are the ones who throw stones at anyone caught laughing about their religion, especially those godless church liberals like me and my friend Charlie.

The almost Reverend Charlie Kraemer did some pretty great things for God's kingdom while he was around. He was one of the funniest people I ever knew within Christendom, and stories about him are legendary. Early one Sunday morning, an elder of the church called Charlie and told him he was sorry that he would not be at worship because he was going bird hunting. Charlie's quick response was, "Any bird that would keep you from worship should be shot!"

Charlie of Charlotte was a funny preacher, but one of the funniest was Jesus of Nazareth. In his first sermon at his home synagogue, he suggested that Syrian lives mattered. He later told stories about how Samaritan lives mattered just as much as Jewish lives. That's not so funny, Jesus. He came to his own people, who received him not, because they thought he was making fun of their religion…blasphemy they called it. The problem for the fuddy-duddies then and now is that is exactly what Jesus was and is doing… making fun of what purports to be religion.

Faith, in the final analysis, is a very funny business. As Ogden Nash so succinctly put it: "How odd of God to choose the Jews." We're always making fun of religion. But religion is fun…tons of fun. It brings laughter and hilarity and hope…it's a way of glorifying God and enjoying our God-given life to the hilt. Maybe laughter is the best vaccine for staying alive and those who laugh may just be the ones who last.

Jesus' close friend, Lazarus, died. And you remember that when "Jesus wept" he coined the shortest verse in scripture. But it wasn't the final word. He raised Lazarus from the dead. The great playwright, Eugene O'Neill captures some of the truth about it in his great work Lazarus Laughed: The third guest recalls the raising of Lazarus: *"Jesus smiled sadly but with tenderness, as one who from a distance of years of sorrows remembers happiness. And then Lazarus knelt and kissed Jesus' feet and both of them smiled and Jesus blessed him and called him "My Brother" and went away; and Lazarus, looking after Him, began to laugh softly like a man in love with God! Such a laugh I never heard! It made my ears drunk!*

*It was like wine! And though I was half-dead with fright, I found myself laughing too!"*

8/23/2020

# Eyes of the Beholders

"Beauty is in the eye of the beholder" is just another way of saying that beauty can be subjective. Jesus of Nazareth taught us that the eye is the "lamp of the body" and insinuates throughout his life that the eye is somehow connected to these hearts of ours for us to figure out truth as well as beauty. One day his disciples asked him why he taught in parables, and he replied that they [his hearers] are blind to the truth that is right before them. "The reason I speak to them in parables is that "seeing they do not perceive, and hearing they do not listen, nor do they understand." They just don't get it!

And who can forget his allusion to the way we see the speck in the neighbor's eye but cannot see the log in our own eye. He really got to us with another kind of eye altogether when he said it would be easier for a camel to go through the "eye" of a needle than for a rich person to get into heaven. Now, he's really meddling with the filthy rich who continually pray "Lord, help me shove this camel".

"You have heard it was said, 'An eye for an eye and a tooth for a tooth... but I say to you, 'Do not resist an evildoer. But if anyone strikes you on the right cheek, turn the other also... You shall love your neighbor and hate your enemy. But I say to you, Love your enemies..." We get it, Jesus, but we can't admit that in the synagogue or church or the public square. Sounds like socialism or something.

Back in the early 1970's, my mission in a Mississippi congregation was to help us through the racial tensions that were ripping at the fabric of community, state and nation. One day, my old Baptist preacher friend, Will Campbell, dropped by my office to check on how things were going. I opened up and let him listen to my frustrations: "I am working so hard to reconcile this racism with reality, but I seem to be butting my head against some wall!"

"Your job is not to reconcile the races," Will calmly explained. "God has already done that; your job is to make the announcement as best you know how."

When someone wipes your blackboard clean like that, we refer to this as an "epiphany" in the religion industry. Brother Campbell showed me clearly that it all depends on your point of view. Your perspective. I was looking at the issue from the dark side of southern racial reality, while he saw the possibilities in the light of the larger gospel truth that this was a done deal to which many turn a deaf ear or a blind eye.

Our worldview might be as different as day and night. We may not see eye to eye, but the cockeyed truth about the dark side of prejudice and bigotry has been exposed as a shame and a sham by Jesus himself. If the childhood song still sings true: "Jesus loves the little children,/ All the children of the world./ Red and yellow, black and white,/ they are precious in his sight....", then he might just be the sight for sore eyes that can help the likes of us behold the beauty of all God's children.

8/30/2020

# Days and Nights of Our Lives

"Like sands through the hourglass, so these are the days of our lives." Those iconic words have introduced a soap opera for what seems like eons, but it's only been around for 55 years, which happens to be long enough in hourglass hours and days of so many lives that mattered enough to maintain their ratings.

Let me invite us all to turn off the television, unplug it, and step outdoors under the canopy of late summer stars and their sister planets. Here we might use our rusty imaginations to think about the days and nights of our own lives. Better yet, let's travel back in time to before the hourglass or sundial were ever invented. But why stop there? Let's go back to the time before there was time. Imagine our shared experiences with those ancient civilizations who realized that there was sunrise and sunset, day and night. No hours yet. They also noticed that the moon in the sky moved in predictable patterns every 30 days or so. People measured longer periods of time in so many "moons". They also realized that every 365 days or so, the sun returned to its original position for its rising and setting at places like Stonehenge.

Had we been around in those ancient nights, our reckoning of the stars in the skies would have been the same as everyone else's. They appeared to move across the dome of the evening sky from the east to the west. They also kept pace with the 365 nights that made up a year back then. Then science marched in one day and claimed a new way of seeing things which would move to a whole new way of believing those things. If such seeing is indeed believing, you'd have to give up your stars in the celestial dome. Try to fathom that the stars were not the ones that were moving, and "the lucky ol' sun was not rolling around heaven all day". What seemed so naturally obvious to the eye of the beholder, was not the case at all.

Writer Lulu Miller describes it like this: "For some, the letting go of the stars was horrifying. It made them feel too small, too pointless, too out of control. They would not believe it. They shot the messengers. When Copernicus gave up the stars, he was condemned as a heretic. When Giordano Bruno gave up the stars, he was burned at the stake… When you give up the stars you get a universe." [Why Fish Don't Exist]

Ever since those wondrous nights of yore, we have had to reimagine our world view and orient our mindset from being the only show in town and the apple of God's eye to realize we live on a tiny blue speck in some backwash of a vast cosmos. It's still hard for some of us, who prefer being more down to earth, to give up our stars floating miraculously across our overhead heavens. In church, for example, folk are still talking about the "creator of heaven and earth", "…descended into hell…ascended into heaven." Or those words in the prayer: "…thy will be done on earth as it is in heaven." Holy writ and revered texts from the world's religions reflect that old version of a three-tiered worldview fit for some museum of antiquity before the big bang exploded into a universe that is beyond the scope of our wildest imagination.

Enough to put us all in orbits for the rest of our livelong days and nights.

9/6/2020

# Asymptomatic

Within this past year of aging as gracefully as I know how, I found out that I had a medical condition unknown to me altogether because it was asymptomatic. I happened to be at a walk-in clinic to check out my ear when they discovered that my heart was broken. I felt as cool as a center seed in a cucumber while my heart was going ninety to nothing. I had no other indicators of my cautious cardiac condition, which was later called atrial fibrillation, or "a-fib" for short. Through the miracle of medication and a procedure called cardioversion, my heart is back to average, or even slightly better than average on good days.

The term "asymptomatic" has crept into our day-to-day jargon as we discuss all the nuances and ramifications of the Covid 19. The term itself can be a condition or a person producing or showing no symptoms of this virus, and the danger in this current situation is that of not knowing exactly who an innocent transmitter of this debilitating pandemic may be. Thus, the necessity of social distancing and face masks and hand washing. Carriers of this contagion are unaware of their own condition.

Running side by side with the pandemic is another human condition that's had latent symptoms for years and years. I grew up a down-home racist and failed to recognize the symptoms of prejudice until halfway through my life. A lot of it was inherited with mother's milk and the southern air that I breathed. Early on, I was indelibly taught by word of mouth and innuendo that all Americans were not created equal and their inalienable rights were not necessarily so. That's why we had signs like "Blacks Only" and voter registration laws. Thanks to some guy by the name of

James Crow, this was "our way of life". All of this was so ingrained in us that I never felt a symptom of the sick attitude that demeans and diminishes other human beings. While taking in all this with my ears and eyes, I never realized that I had a broken heart and closed mind.

Then, one day, I woke up and realized that my lily-white heart was not in the right place. I was sick without ever realizing it because of the asymptomatic nature of this prejudicial plague. There's no vaccine for this, but the cure comes with our doing the hard work of reconciliation. In the dog days of this Covid-19 virus, the racial issue has raised its tired hand once again for resolution and justice. We might have fooled ourselves into believing that sort of stuff has gone with the wind. But it hasn't. And it won't until we acknowledge that we have this contagious infirmity even while seemingly asymptomatic and passing this weakness of the heart to another generation.

As Benjamin Franklin foretold us: "Justice will not be served until those who are unaffected are as outraged as those who are." It's a good time to whip this ancient dragon by listening to these words by the late Thurgood Marshall: "We must dissent from indifference. We must dissent from apathy. We must dissent from the fear, the hatred, and the mistrust... We must dissent because America can do better, because America has no choice but to do better."

9/13/2020

# You Must Remember This...

...a kiss is just a kiss, on that you can rely..." Those lovely lyrics from the the classic song "As Time Goes By" have been a haunting reminder of something that's missing in our lives during these pandemic days. I'm good and ready to take off this kiss-proof mask and spin the bottle toward the good old days of simple affections. A kiss is a rich symbol of more than puckered lips applied to other lips or cheeks, but when will we ever get to kiss even the poet's "joy as it flies"? Or to paraphrase the Psalmist: "How long, Oh Lord, will this crazy contagion continue?"

Even if we grew up in low-on-affection households, we remember those parental kisses that put us to bed or sent us to school. And we remember when those kisses by those same parents became somewhat embarrassing when we had grown to that inept period in our adolescence when we were sneaking around to steal a kiss in childhood innocence. And surely, we can recall those first kisses that told of a passion too wonderful for mere words.

If you check it out, you'll find a lot of kissing going on in the Bible, and not just in the Song of Solomon. Patriarchs were always kissing their sons as part of the blessing from one generation to another. Jonathan and David kissed each other farewell. Who can forget the sensual display of passion when that nameless woman who is simply called a "sinner" in Luke's gospel anoints Jesus' feet with ointment and kisses them? We all remember that kiss of death which Judas used to designate Jesus to the Roman soldiers.

Paul employs a unique phrase in several of his letters to the young churches: "Greet one another with a holy kiss." No biblical scholar has expounded on that phrase to a great extent, and very few churches include kissing in the worship service. Back in the 1970's churches went through a "hugging phase", greeting everyone who entered the vestibule with holy hugs! Those who were shy felt a bit uncomfortable when accosted by a hug-seeking usher. The display of public affection just seemed out of place when carried to extreme.

Maybe there's a time and place for stealing a little sacred kiss if this kiss-free curse called Covid ever leaves us alone. Our hope is that the fundamental things still apply as time goes by even during times like these. When we kiss someone, there's something almost holy about it. Whether we are kissing away the tears of a dear friend or tucking our children into their beds, we mean by that kiss a kind of tangible prayer. When our lips reach out to touch another, we are placing a holy hope on the tie that binds us and sealing it with a kiss.

9/20/2020

# Forgive Us Our Ubiquitous Words

Remember those awkward collisions of somewhat sacred words when worshippers from different backgrounds tried to blend their versions of Jesus' prayer: "forgive us our *#*%@ as we forgive those who #*%&@* against us…" At least, that's what it sounded like as "debts and debtors" took on "trespasses and those who trespass against us…"

This war of the words can easily distract us from the substance of the utterances. Somewhat like that preacher who began the sermon with these words: "While we are here for an hour to worship, 240 children will die of starvation, and we won't give a damn." When the gasp subsided, the minister asked them which was more offensive: that he had used a "bad" word or that those children had died from our indifference.

These words asking God to forgive our debts and/or trespasses come right out of Jesus' background of observing Yom Kippur, the Day of Atonement. Here's where we all strip ourselves of our own righteousness before God and beg for mercy and forgiveness for all we have done wrong or left undone. Out here in the far country, we confess our misery on the way home to the prodigal Father who runs halfway down the driveway to embrace us back into the fold.

The hardest part of all comes with the "as we forgive our debtors and/or those who have trespassed against us…" Jesus pushes us take on the proactive form of faith that turns the other cheek, goes the second mile, and does not return evil for evil, but takes thought for what is noble in the sight of all. Being forgiven does not automatically transform us into forgiving people.

Here's where gospel encounters our prejudices against those who are unlike us. Jesus dares us to love our enemies and to see the good even in those we think disdainful so that we are free to live on the upside of atonement and appreciate the "other." Rather than our benign neglect for those 240 children or our indifference toward those black lives seeking some semblance of equal justice under the law, we turn the words of our mouths and the meditations of our hearts into deeds of compassion as God has been compassionate with the likes of us. And this leads us to a hope so desperately needed in our current disparity.

Just days before her death, Anne Frank wrote in her diary: "… in spite of everything I still believe that people are really good at heart… I see the world gradually being turned into a wilderness, I hear the ever-approaching thunder, which will destroy us too, I can feel the sufferings of millions and yet, if I look up into the heavens, I think it will all come right, that this cruelty too will end, and that peace and tranquility will return again."

Justice Ruth Bader Ginsburg died on the eve of Rosh Hashana, the Jewish new year. Fittingly, it was a day when Jews look backward and forward, reflecting on what has passed, and preparing for what is to come. Justice Ginsburg's death marks the end of her long battle on behalf of equality for all Americans. She deserves all the honor and respect we can muster as a nation of many faiths and creeds.

Yom Kippur begins tonight at sundown. In our current wilderness full of pandemic and racial unrest and all the religious and political shams and shenanigans going on right now, we could surely use the power of repentance and forgiveness while taking thought for what is noble in the sight of all like Anne Frank and RBG did in their beautiful lifetimes. Shalom.

9/27/2020

# Simple Things Matter a Great Deal

Andre Dubus had stopped to help a woman and a man stranded on the side of a highway when he was hit by a passing car. He saved the woman's life by throwing her out of the way, but he lost one of his legs and spent the rest of his life in a wheelchair. Dubus was a college professor of creative writing and an author of many good short stories; as a result of that incident he said, "Some of my characters now feel more grateful about simple things — breathing, buying groceries, sunlight — because I do."

Some folks find themselves holding on for dear life after some tragedy deals them more than they think they can possibly handle. They shift into survival mode in order to just get through the day. They adapt to the motions of living but fail to find happiness or affection. When their lives come to an end, the cause of death might simply read: "failure to survive." By the way, Dubus once quipped that the reason he wrote was "that he didn't want to die before he was dead."

The current pandemic has put the fear of God in many of us, and we try to be on guard from getting it or transmitting it to others. We wash our hands and keep our distance. Some say wearing masks infringes upon our freedom, which is "just another word for nothing left to lose". Others of us realize that it's such a simple and respectful way of lowering contagious risks that have killed over 200,000 of our citizens so far. Surely, we have come to realize that if we take life as a gift for all to enjoy, then we see through the smoke screens of fear to a better reality based on a simplicity that matters most of all. Or as the old hymn aptly paints the upside of this catch 22: *'twas grace that taught my heart to fear and grace my fears relieved…*

Perhaps nothing says it better than that old Shaker song: *Tis the gift to be simple, 'tis the gift to be free/ 'Tis the gift to come down where we ought to be,/ And when we find ourselves in the place just right, 'Twill be in the valley of love and delight./ When true simplicity is gained,/ To bow and to bend we shan't be ashamed,/ To turn, turn 'twill be our delight,/ Till by turning, turning we come 'round right.*

On this side of the grave, we examine our own failure to be and achieve what we set out so confidently to do and to be. How we pray to God to give us power that we can overcome the problems ourselves. Just this week we realized that even the most prominent people in the world can become susceptible to a virus that is no respecter of one's position or power.

Maybe now we will realize that we can't ride out the storms of life on our own strength, no matter how much we have. As Andre puts it: "We don't have to live great lives, we just have to understand and survive the one we've got." In theological terms, what we really need — and have needed all along — is the grace to appreciate those simple gifts of goodness and mercy that have been following us all our livelong days.

10/4/2020

# Pumpkins, Posters & Politics

While the days grow shorter, fall colors are carousing with our natural surroundings. No, the leaves haven't turned their bright orange or brilliant red yet, but the highways are scattered with political posters as candidates change their colors for this special season. Elections bring out all sorts of flamboyant characters, each claiming to stand in that great tradition for truth, justice and the American way. Well, maybe just the American way, whatever that may be these days when truth and justice seem so elusive to so many of our citizens. Republicans and Democrats strut their banners and sling their slogans throughout the landscapes urging voters to consider their quintessential qualifications.

In the middle of the everchanging plethora of signs, Mother Nature exposes her constant reminders that outlasts all the campaign rhetoric: fresh pumpkins ripe for carving into jack-o-lanterns; tired peach trees; exhausted corn stalks. Silent skies interrupted by honking Canadian geese letting us know they are heading south "ere the winter storms begin." Crisp weather contrasts with the summer heat, and our air conditioners look forward to their winter hibernation.

No wonder the campaign signs that litter our roads don't catch our attention. While we may look at them occasionally, we are always looking beyond them to the vivid messages sent to us by a world that is always changing, but always faithful in its promise to support our living with gifts that come with the territory. Around us, all nature sings the old covenant tune that God promised to

Noah and his descendants: "While the earth remains, seedtime and harvest, cold and heat, summer and winter, day and night, shall not cease." It's hard to match the campaign promise like that one.

Maybe this is the proper setting for our billboards persuading us to vote for this or that candidate, who are like the leaves of grass in Isaiah's vision: "All flesh is grass, and all its beauty is like the flower of the field. The grass withers, the flower fades..." Jesus picked up the same melody when he spoke of the lilies of the field and claimed that even King Solomon, the wisest political officer of Israel, couldn't hold a candle to this kind of simple symbol of God's faithfulness. Maybe voters will catch a glimpse of this quiet grandeur of God surrounding all those posters and realize just how temporary our political wisdom is at best and how tentative our human efforts are at their worst. "Put not your trust in princes," says the psalmist. "When his breath departs he returns to the earth; on that very day his plans perish."

Don't misunderstand. I am very passionate about the idea that politics are important, and we have a serious obligation to vote our consciences. It is our way of demonstrating the essence of democracy that if human beings are sacred, then they are surely equal. Hopefully, our consciences are always being informed and reformed by the one who, through the power of politics, was executed with other criminals on a cross. What a reminder of an everlasting campaign promise: love that overcomes hate; peace that overcomes war; and a compassionate God that so loved this world of ours with all its pumpkins, posters and people.

10/11/2020

# We're Not Jewish; We're Southern!

When they were nine and six, our oldest grandchildren were discussing religion around the kitchen table. Their mother was a family counselor for the large Jewish Community Center in Charlotte, so she enjoyed the various holidays of that faith. Since this family had yet to find a "church home", religion was a confusing topic at times. So Cooper raises a question at the table: "Mom, are we Jewish?" Having just observed Christmas and Hanukkah, of course the kid was confused. While his mother was trying to explain it all, his very wise sister Claire exclaimed in exasperation, "Cooper, we are not Jewish; we're southern!"

The combination of those words — Jewish and southern — felt right at home with me. Fate and faith combined their forces on me early along by letting me grow up in a neighborhood full of wonderful Jewish folk who had settled in our town as immigrants to this country from eastern Europe and Ukraine. The Kaplans and Rosens and Goodmans lived next door or across the street and shared their lives with us in many ways. One night they let me ask the childhood question before the Passover Seder "Why is this night so different than any other?" Rabbi Blumenthal was one of my daily newspaper subscribers, and I hand-delivered the Clarion Ledger to his second-floor room at the Trolio Hotel. The local Synagogue was still active in the days of my youth but has vanished into the evolving diaspora over time.

During my early ministry, I cherished and maintained my relationship with the Jewish community. While I could not wrangle him the invitation to pray over high school football games like a protestant, the rabbi and I enjoyed tennis and sharing services on

Fridays and Sundays. We opened our fellowship meals with our congregations and taught our youth the elements of each faith. In my last parish in West End, we welcomed several Jewish neighbors to worship with us since there were no places of worship for them in our vicinity. When the new synagogue was established, the interim rabbi was my age and had grown up southern about twenty miles south of my hometown. We instituted an interfaith worship Thanksgiving service with other congregations that would eventually welcome Buddhists, and Muslims in the area.

Antisemitism has a long history of horror and can take many scary turns. The great reformer Martin Luther's outrage against the Jews in Germany set the stage for Adolf Hitler's manifesto and the Holocaust. I never knew what it was until I heard a Baptist preacher in our town include the term "Christ killing Jews" in his prayer. The Klan had bombed the synagogue in my second parish in Mississippi, reiterating the senseless sentiment. As if we don't have enough to say grace over these days, we must face the resurging threat of Christian nationalism that's linked with white supremacy challenging the sanctity of religious freedom in this country.

According to the gospels, Jesus suggests that religious freedom should not be used as a political weapon that incites hatred and bigotry to bash the downtrodden or those other poor losers, but to feed the hungry, give water to the thirsty, clothing to the naked, provide universal medical care for the sick, visit the prisoners, and taking care of the immigrants and other strangers. In the letter to the church in Galatia, we discover that "There is no longer Jew or Greek, there is no longer slave or free, there is no longer male and female; for all of you are one in Christ Jesus. And if you belong to Christ, then you are Abraham's offspring, heirs according to the promise." Shalom, y'all!

10/18/2020

# Marvelous Mary of Mannsdale

The black and beautiful life of Mary Goins mattered to a multitude of my people. She lived every inch of her life with a gracious dignity that made it so easy for all of us to love and respect her. She was born a slave as the Civil War erupted in 1861 and died in what was purported to be freedom in 1961, when she was a hundred. She was a native of Mannsdale, Mississippi, and never left.

She lived on Granddaddy's place up that short path past those haystacks on a pole. The house was both delightful and dilapidated with a small porch on the front where she would sit and wile away her countless days. From that vantage point she could see the Bennett house and remember when it was brand spanking new, when she was just thirty-nine at the turn of the 20th century. She was there when their first born, Dudley, died as a child. Mary was sixty-six when our grandmother died, and she would end up as the multi-tasking matriarch in charge of rearing my mother and her brood of siblings.

An old pot-bellied stove was the centerpiece of the two-roomed shanty. The front room served as den and bedroom, and I remember that all the walls and ceilings were covered with the funny papers. [I later learned that by pasting and layering newspaper to the wall, the house was more insulated against the fierce winds of winter.] When Mary welcomed me and the other cousins, we felt in our bones we were almost kin — like stray grandchildren. She would let us jump on the single cot and give us a hot sweet potato from the stove. The back room was somewhat of a kitchen, bordered by a small back porch leading to the outhouse.

Mary Goins seemed an enigma to me. She was almost alien yet as close as family itself. In spite of the content of her caring character, the color of her skin set her apart. But not that far apart. To hear our parents speak of Mary and her kind…including ol' Frank Bennett and Joe…you'd think we all came from the same stock. If the truth be admitted, we did. Like Dilsey was to the Compson family in Faulkner's <u>The Sound and the Fury</u>, Mary not only endured but she prevailed somehow by God's grace.

Since the early 1800's in Mississippi, the years and the place had created a tapestry full of all sorts of people doing their parts to survive and keep faith going from one generation to another. Our great grandfather would live through his days in the Confederacy. Our grandfather and his new bride would set up housekeeping in the new house in 1900, and Mary and her kind would be essential to whatever life would hold for them as they dared to have the children who would someday give birth to the likes of us. She could look out from her porch and see the generations parading up and down the path till Kingdom come. She knew in her bones the disparity of plantation capitalism that would build this nation's economy, but she could prayerfully picture a new day dawning for the generations coming when her people could be full citizens.

My simple way of honoring this beautiful and saintly lady in my life is affirming that black lives mattered a great deal back then and continue to matter more than this world ever dreams of.

10/25/2020

# God's Reputation Is on the Line, Again

Piety and pride can do terrible harm, but they can also create enormous messes when combined with politics. The looming elections have us all in tail tizzies, but once again the hard-core Christians seem to have it all under control with their god.

Back in the 2008 presidential elections, I was especially intrigued by what happened during that campaign at a rally in Davenport, Iowa, when Rev. Arnold Conrad offered this invocation: *I would also pray Lord, that your reputation is involved in all that happens between now and November, because there are millions of people around this world praying to their God — whether it's Hindu, Buddha, Allah — that his [McCain's] opponent wins for a variety of reasons. And Lord I pray that you would guard your own reputation, because they're going to think that their god is bigger than you, if that happens. So I pray that you would step forward and honor your own name in all that happens between now and Election Day.*

Before I heard that prayer, I had never realized that God might have a reputation. After that particular election, of course, one might have to conclude that God's reputation was shot to hell. When you think about it, throughout the various histories of humanity, the reputation of one god is pitted against the reputation of another...depending on who is telling the story as to which god "outgods" the other.

For some reason, people just can't fathom that the love of God might be bigger than a god who simply champions their particular religion or race or nation or way of seeing the world. The kind of bumper sticker mentality of "God Bless America" as if no other country in the world ever matters to God.

I'm sure the god of the minister in Davenport, Iowa, would not want God to smear God's holy name by abandoning those most precious voters during that election. After all, the real Christians are deserving of their right to win — whether it's a war or an election — in order to preserve truth, virtue, white supremacy, and the "real" American way of life. One nation under God...God bless America...in God we trust...and all that sort of thing. But there's a fly in the ointment, and it's not God's reputation on the block here at all.

Jesus talks about God who has a reputation for being extremely inclusive, which most righteous people — like our reverend from Iowa — find unacceptable. But that is exactly how God is. Everyone is included, no one left out. God is not satisfied that just a few of God's favorite children might be saved; God wants them all, Jew and Gentile, slave and free, board chairman and garbage collector, president and prostitute, rich and wretched, visiting foreign dignitaries and illegal aliens, the right-wing pro-lifers and bleeding-heart liberals.

"In a society that is growing radically more secular every day," writes David Brooks, "I'd say we have more to fear from political dogmatism than religious dogmatism. We have more to fear from those who let their politics determine their faith practices and who turn their religious communities into political armies. We have more to fear from people who look to politics as a substitute for faith." "Politics needs a reference point outside of politics," argues the Hebrew University religious philosopher Moshe Halbertal. "It needs values, it needs facts and it needs leaders who respect that there is a sacred domain of decisions that will never be used to promote political gain, only the common good."

11/1/2020

# What Counts the Most?

A lot counting has been going on over the past few days as this country elected its 46th President. Democracy is built upon counting the ballots of its citizens and the whole notion that each vote counts. The race for the White House became a cliffhanger and a nailbiter over the past few days while five states seemed to take their ever-loving time in the counting process. In the political struggle leading up to the election some of the rhetoric became dicey and desperate. Forget that old campaign vision of a "kinder and gentler" democracy where all voters are respected and considerate to each other. It's dog eat dog in the fight to the finish.

Adages abound when it comes to understanding what counts the most in these circumstances and in life itself: "It's not who wins or loses, but how you play the game." "It's not who finished first; it's how you run the race." We live under the illusion that the one who ends up with the most stuff before death, wins. If it's the thought that really counts — God forbid — then perish the thoughts that have led us to think the way we do in this current culture.

Speaking of dog-eat-dog, one of the finest preachers of our time is Fred Craddock, and his story about a greyhound dog teaches us all a new trick when it comes to seeing what might count after all. Here's how he tells it...

"I was in a home not long ago where they had adopted a dog that had been a racer. It was a big old greyhound, spotted hound, lying there in the den. One of the kids in the family, just a toddler, was pulling on its tail, and a little older kid had his head over on that dog's stomach, used it for a pillow. That dog just seemed so happy and I said to the dog, 'uh, are you still racing any?'

'No, no, no, I don't race anymore.'

I said, 'do you miss the glitter and excitement of the track?'

He said, 'No, no.'

I said, 'well, what's the matter? You got too old?'

'No, no, I still had some race in me.'

'Well, did you not win?'

He said, 'I won over a million dollars for my owner.'

'Then what was it, bad treatment?'

'Oh no, they treated us royally when we were racing.'

I said, 'Then what? Did you get crippled?'

He said, 'No, no, no.'

I said, 'Then what?'

And he said, 'I quit.'

I said, 'why did you quit?'

And he said, 'I discovered that what I was chasing was not really a rabbit. And I quit.' He looked at me and said, 'All that running, running, running, running, and what I was chasing was not even real.'"

Could we learn a new trick or two from such an old and wise dog? Maybe what we've been chasing recently is just not the real thing but a figment of someone's false imagination as to what makes this a great nation after all. "Touched by the better angels of our nature", can we be counted on to do what's right by honoring both the process and the President-elect in order to heal all our hurts and become that "sweet land of liberty" once again?

11/8/2020

# Losing Our Religion

Over the past few months, I have come as near as I ever have to losing what was left of my religion. This pandemic is beginning to wear thin, and the recent election was thick with thieves full of all sorts of chicanery, negative ads and stonewalling the outcomes. Good news has come: we just might have a vaccine before we can say the Apostles' Creed, and the voters have made their choice for a new President crystal clear. There is a God!

A lot of people have lost their religion over a lot of things, but have you ever considered what would happen if a minister lost his or her religion. When I worked at the preacher's trade for so many years, I worried about losing it. It is possible, you know. One minister I know confessed that he almost lost his during the ninth month of a six-month building project at his church!

When we moved within driving range of Pinehurst, all my friends who indulged in that holy game called golf would offer the next interrogatory sentence: "You do play golf, don't you?" My comeback was always "I tried it once and almost lost my religion. Without that I would be out of work." But the worst possible scenario would be to lose your faith in church! I came within a fraction of falling out with faith altogether in several of those ungodly church meetings.

I recall a conversation with an insurance agent in which I asked about the possibility of insuring ministers from the loss of their religion. Virtuoso pianist and violinist have their hands insured. Jimmy Durante had his nose insured. Why shouldn't preachers have their religion insured since it has something to do with their livelihood as well as their vocational calling.

But why stop with just the professionals of the church? Why not offer insurance packages for those in the pew against that doomful day when everything falls apart. When there's no reason for going on. When all is lost. When a pandemic comes along, and the church doors are locked.

Some will argue that religion is a kind of insurance. It's a way to hedge your bets. "Let's join a religion, just in case there is a god who can help us make it through this mess." Others even consider it a form of everlasting life insurance: if we believe in the right religion, say the right things, follow the rules, we will be guaranteed a first-class ticket on the train bound for the sweet, bye and bye. And may the devil take the hindmost! I've known people who feel this way, and I almost lose my religion whenever I'm around them.

Maybe it's a good thing to lose our religion. When you finally hear the Good News, you might discover that it draws the curtain on the whole charade of religion as we know it. The Gospel simply announces that all those things that the human race thought it had to do to get right with God — like believing, behaving, worshipping, sacrificing, and trusting God as hard as we can and saying so by putting that on our money — none of those things ever had a chance of doing the trick when our only purpose is to enjoy a God who loves us religiously and won't lose us. Ever.

11/15/2020

# Those Gallant Ghosts of Gettysburg

This Thursday past marked the date [in 1863] of Lincoln's most poignant address in memory of all those soldiers who gave the last full measure of their devotion on that particular and decisive field of battle. More than just another fall day on that sacred place, that day's memorial service represented the hopes and fears of a nation still hurting from the ravages of death and destruction that broke the very fabric of our faith in each other.

This beleaguered yet resilient country is now a band of wandering pilgrims on our way to celebrate its annual Thanksgiving in quite an uncanny fashion. We are dismayed and distraught by the fact that, so far, over 250,000 of our fellow citizens have died from the Covid 19 pandemic since its inception in the spring. We are a people filled with suspicious fear and hatred and anger who just endured another election to save our ailing democracy but with little seeming change or affect. No one seems to want to give any part of their devotion or decency for a common good beyond ourselves. While we may not be at war, we are certainly less than civil toward each other, and it's killing us each and every day.

How can we find the spiritual traction and human gumption that will enable us to find a glimmer of truth with enough hope in it to meet the challenges? While a vaccine that will offer us some form of immunity from this awful pandemic looks promising, what can we do to rebuild the trust necessary for our life together when simply wearing a facemask for the safety of all concerned is considered divisive? What can heal us and restore our collective soul? Maybe we need to hear anew old John Donne's notion that "no one is an island. Each is a piece of the continent, a part of the main. Each person's death diminishes me for I am involved in all of humanity. Therefore, send not to know for whom the bell tolls, it tolls for thee."

Lincoln's plea then seems so appropriate for this dark hour in America's struggle. Instead of the strewn bodies of soldiers on Gettysburg's killing fields, we might convert those daily numbers of Covid victims and health care workers into a monument of grace and prayer to God and hear anew these very Presidential words reframing our moment in history by telling us the truth about ourselves: *It is for us the living, rather, to be dedicated here to the unfinished work which they who fought here have thus far so nobly advanced. It is rather for us to be here dedicated to the great task remaining before us — that from these honored dead we take increased devotion to that cause for which they gave the last full measure of devotion — that we here highly resolve that these dead shall not have died in vain — that this nation, under God, shall have a new birth of freedom — and that government of the people, by the people, for the people, shall not perish from the earth.*

11/22/2020

# Turning Down the Noise

Maybe it's because these new hearing aids really do their job, but I've noticed how loud we've become as a country and a culture. I'm not just talking about used politicians. Rather, I am referring to all the gizmos and gadgets that are now part of our landscaping arsenals.

THE NEW YORKER

Take this fall season when the autumn leaves drift by our windows, those autumn leaves of red and gold forming some kind of unwanted nuisance on our yards and driveways. Such a season invites us to sit on our patios and porches to enjoy nature showing off her multi-colored tapestries. Suddenly, you realize that your conversations are helplessly drowned under a cacophonous calliope of roaring leaf blowers ricocheting off the pine trees or wafting across the lake.

"I will now play a familiar seasonal piece"

Where in the world did these loud monsters designed to blow hot air and break wind come from? I'm sure that some great venture capitalist devised these things with a utilitarian purpose void of any consideration for the noise pollution they create. Every day, trailers drawn by loud pickups unload their mowers and blowers to do battle with such a formidable foe as nature itself, using a lot of sound and fury to signify silence overkill. The war zone is not confined to refined areas of nice houses. Go to shopping centers and parking lots where those trailers unload their mercenaries of leaf and litter removals. Their boots are on the ground from sunup to sundown.

 Several years ago I enjoyed being in a group of folk touring China where something seemed strangely missing as we went about the villages and cities and countryside. After a while, it occurred to me that there were no blowers making their ungodly rackets in the streets or shops or open areas. Older women and men were utilizing homemade brooms without motors to keep the country as clean as a whistle while being as quiet as a mouse. I watched my good friend and retired peach grower, Watts Auman, quietly sweep the Great Wall of China.

Even though such tranquility was made in China, where else might one find some hint of noiselessness in this world? If you head into the big block stores for Black Friday wearing your Covid 19 masks, you might want to stuff some cotton in your ears to blunt the loudest version of Christmas music ever perpetuated on human eardrums. Jesus himself wouldn't be caught dead in such a musical megalomania. The roar of the blowers in the parking lot seems more pleasing than the "Angels from the Realms of Glory" blaring at you in the checkout lines.

Meanwhile, we all wait for that eerie Eve when "…silently the wondrous gift is given" in order to tune our heart strings to the more delicate decibels of December. Who knows, instead of beating our swords into plowshares or spears into pruning hooks, we may have to abandon our leaf blowers to take up the soft whispering sounds of brooms to sweep away everything in order for us all to sleep in heavenly peace and quiet.

11/29/2020

# The Insight of Hindsight

"Today is the tomorrow that you worried about yesterday" proclaimed the cross-stitch sign in the dentist's office. That'll make your brain itch. While you're scratching your head about it, here's another way to consider time: "Today will be the yesterday you'll try to forget about tomorrow."

We are forever living existentially between our hindsight and our foresight. If we could measure our hindsight, we would probably all have 20/20 vision. And we use such sight to discover who we are. I am the accumulation of years of experiences. My character is formulated by the building blocks of days and years of choices made and people known and books read and events that occurred. Through this process, I began to obtain wisdom from all the failures as well as the successes of bygone days.

Some things in our past are best forgotten, but the forgetting mechanism in our psyche doesn't always work. We are stuck with our mistakes, even though they are not the stuff of the stories we recount to our children about the good old days. We prefer to recall those brief shining moments of the Camelots we've experienced rather than the sloughs of despond that muddied our feet. Thus we work at assimilating our weaker moments and bad judgements and moral mistakes into a kind of quasi persona that really isn't our true selves.

After several years of playing "If only I had…", we bar the doors of the past, shut the windows of pain and betrayal in order to experience a form of myopia which allows us to live with ourselves in spite of our memory. When we short-circuit our hindsight in such ways, we develop nearsightedness that doesn't see too far beyond the immediate struggle to maintain our own equilibrium. And we develop shortsightedness about the future. We lose the vision that used to give us hope and courage. We discover the wisdom of the prophet that a people without a vision soon perish. We become very perishable persons, unable to cope with the slings and arrows of any misfortune past, present or future.

This pandemic seems to have caught the whole world off guard, and we are hard pressed to admit we knew in January that this was going to hit us hard. Illusions were spread throughout this land that this too would pass by spring, while another reality was biting us in the derriere so that today we are languishing as lambs to the slaughter. From the beginning, there was this lack of a vision — foresight derived from insight — that could have saved so many people and healed our lagging spirits. In retrospect, it's quite easy to see that our political leaders became shortsighted and lacked any form of conviction and courage to do what was right.

One of the functions of faith is to give us insight: insight from outside ourselves yet very much about ourselves, about living with others, about the world itself, about God, about grace. The amazing grace we used to sing about down at the church is rich with all kind of wisdom for the living of these days. Its sweetness is more than just how it sounds to the ears. It is also sweet to the eyes. "I once was lost, but now am found, Was blind, but now I see." And it has farsighted and everlasting tendencies: "When we've been there ten thousand years, bright shining as the sun, we've no less days to sing God's praise than when we first begun."

12/6/2020

# Worshipping the Ground
# on Which We Walk

When we worship the ground we walk on, the route is not that infamous road paved with good intentions nor the primrose path. Not even memory lane nor the yellow brick road to Oz. Rather, the basic surmise here is that of ordinary *terra firma*. However, there's something magical about this common ground when one develops a reverence for it and those special people in our lives who tread thereupon.

It's one of those terms of endearment we use almost too casually. "He just worships the ground she walks on" assumes an infatuation with the beautiful and adorned one. The ground is merely the stage upon which, to use the words of Lord Byron, **"She walks in beauty like the night/ Of cloudless climes and starry skies;/ and all the best of dark and bright/ Meet in the aspect of her eyes..."**

But let's get back down to earth by taking a hike, which is a great way to worship the ground on which you happen to be walking, even though it can put a hex on certain aspects of such an noble endeavor. A recent stroll in the Blue Ridge this fall forced me to constantly watch the path with rocks and roots hidden beneath the covering of colorful leaves. This concentration did not allow me to look around at the other flora and fauna nor the sky above. Throw in the notion that I saw a delightful waterfall which needed photographing while the rest of the group began to disappear up the river gorge far from sight.

"Stumbling Over Stardust" implies a hike of sorts, and many a time the operative word is "stumbling", as in falling flat on your aspect of thine own eyes while losing your pride. Like that time when Alice unsuspectingly fell into a rabbit hole and discovered a whole wonderland!

At our best we are all accidental tourist making our way on the sacred journey in the search for meaning. The only thing really certain is the ground itself. The good earth. Our holy ground.

Out there, on Mount Horeb, Moses — working for his father-in-law as a temporary shepherd and on the run for a murder charge — happened to see what appeared to be fire in his peripheral vision and turned aside to see this sight for sore eyes. Before he had a chance to beat around the bush, this strange voice started talking: "Moses, I wouldn't come any closer. Take off those Birkenstocks because you are standing on holy ground." And that's when Moses got the word to worship the ground he was walking on because you never know whether you are in the presence of Yahweh in what appears to be only an asbestos shrub.

The guiding light of this blogging enterprise are the words from novelist Marilynne Robinson, urging us to see the paths of stardust on which we are walking worshippers: *"I have spent my life watching, not to see beyond the world, merely to see, great mystery, what is plainly before my eyes. I think the concept of transcendence is based on a misreading of the creation. With all respect to heaven, the scene of the miracle is here, among us."* The new writer on the block, Lulu Miller, puts an existential twist on it like this: **"Nowhere is the sky so blue, the grass so green, the sunshine so bright, the** *shade so welcome, as right here, now, today... There is a grandeur in this view of life...if you can't see it, shame on you."*

12/13/2020

# Waiting for the Hallelujah Chorus

George Frideric Handel was a musical stranger until I started singing in our college choir. Maybe we had met earlier, but his name just didn't ring a bell like it would when we joined with the Jackson Symphony Orchestra each December to sing the "Messiah". My infatuation with Handel's major oratorio finds me still humming from this work every Christmas season. "For unto us a child is born...and the government shall be upon his shoulders and his name shall be called wonderful, counselor, the mighty God...the Prince of Peace."

If you are familiar with the entire work, you will know that it contains selected King James [James VI of Scotland and/or James I of the British Empire where the sun never set] versions depicting the birth, death and resurrection of Jesus. Typical performances of the whole thing could take nearly three hours, which is why our annual December endeavor only dealt with the stories of Jesus' birth. Even so, the classical endeavor was rather lengthy, and you could hardly wait for the grand finale to be sung: the "Hallelujah Chorus". To the audience it finally meant a welcomed chance to stand for this triumphant crescendo for a variety of reasons: a] it's what King George II did at the first performance; b] the dynamic of the music demands they stand; or c] to relieve their tired rumps from sitting so long.

When you reflect deeply about the message and meaning of the Hallelujah Chorus, you realize it has yet to become close to reality as we know it. It's more akin to whistling "Dixie", for which white southerners stood whenever and wherever it was played. The mighty Messiah libretto declares that "the kingdom of this world is become the kingdom of our Lord and of his Christ, and he shall reign forever and ever and ever…" Last time I checked, this crazy place is a long way from being ruled by the Lord, and his Christ. Hardly any evidence of a collective ethic resembling the teachings of Jesus, royalty to the contrary notwithstanding.

Once the dust settled on Jesus' birth and life among us, the kingdoms of this world — beginning with Charlemagne and the Holy Roman Empire — realized that cozying up to this Messiah thing could pay political and economic dividends. From then on, empires and/or kingdoms conveniently declared themselves to be a Christian nation or whatever in order to maintain control over any other adversaries — real or imagined. Thus, the holy catholic church and the communion of the saints became duped and used for everything under the sun except living out the Gospel truth of the Prince of Peace.

All of this, of course, has prevented the sacred dream of the Hallelujah Chorus from ever becoming reality. Maybe we can wait for an act of congress which would take from here to kingdom come. Or…, while we sit on our duffs waiting for the Hallelujah Chorus to come true, we might as well join in John Lennon's counterculture song: "Imagine there's no countries/ It isn't hard to do/ nothing to kill or die for/ and no religion too/ imagine all the people living life in peace…" I think we might be able to Handle such a dream that's more strangely akin to the Messiah's vision of peace on earth and goodwill to all, as "in all people that on earth do dwell sing to the Lord with cheerful voice…" Imagine that. Hallelujah!

12/20/2020

# To Dream an Impossible World

In the short yet endangered history of western civilization as we know it, religion and politics became the strangest of bedfellows as empires and kingdoms feuded over whichever god would best serve their cause. Rome was the first to misuse this power. Luther upset the applecart in the Reformation. Henry VIII did it in jolly old England for a divorce. Hitler did it as part of his holocaust endeavor. Even the good ol' USofA [founded on the notion that there will be "NO established religion"] employed King James' version of holy writ to justify slavery and still misuses the remnants of racism to undergird pride and prejudice. The same Holy Bible awkwardly held by our President in front of a church as a photo op in his campaign for reelection.

Growing up Protestant, I can remember being taught to hate Roman Catholics who were vilified by the term "papist", and that President Kennedy had a hotline to the Vatican. As we enter a brand new year, let's be glad there's a smidgen of hope that the people of faith can speak truth to power. As the Covid 19 pandemic continues to take its awful toll, Pope Francis spoke to the hopes and fears of all the years when he wrote these simple and prophetic words: *This is a moment to dream big, to rethink our priorities — what we value, what we want, what we seek — and to commit to act in our daily life on what we have dreamed of.*

*God asks us to dare to create something new. We cannot return to the false securities of the political and economic systems we had before the crisis. We need economies that give to all access to the fruits of creation, to the basic needs of life: to land, lodging and labor. We need a politics that can integrate and dialogue with*

211

*the poor, the excluded and the vulnerable, that gives people a say in the decisions that affect their lives. We need to slow down, take stock and design better ways of living together on this earth.*

*To come out of this crisis better, we have to recover the knowledge that as a people we have a shared destination. The pandemic has reminded us that no one is saved alone. What ties us to one another is what we commonly call solidarity. Solidarity is more than acts of generosity, important as they are; it is the call to embrace the reality that we are bound by bonds of reciprocity. On this solid foundation we can build a better, different, human future.*

Some folk might dismiss such rhetoric as ecclesiastical hubris or just wishful thinking from another old white man in a funny hat. Others of us hear in these words the basic teachings of a young rabbi whose birthday we just celebrated. He spoke about nations that take care the hungry, the thirsty, the naked, and the incarcerated, concluding that when countries care about "the least of these who are members of my family," they care about him. Who in heaven's name does Jesus think he is espousing that kind of madness with the whimsical naivete akin to Don Quixote?

Spanish philosopher and creator of the *Man of La Mancha,* Miguel de Cervantes, expresses this conundrum: *"When life itself seems lunatic, who knows where madness lies?*

*Perhaps to be too practical is madness. To surrender dreams — this may be madness. Too much sanity may be madness — and maddest of all: to see life as it is, and not as it should be!"*

12/27/2020

# When Our Memory Is Our Future

"You show promise." Do you remember when someone told you that? It may have been a teacher or a coach. Some other adult you respected in your growing years. I can't pinpoint the memory in my own mind, but the phrase swirled around me, caught hold and pulled me toward the future with more hope. I had almost forgotten about it, until I heard it recently. Suddenly, time-released capsules of images exploded in little visions of all those in my past who said that to me. Maybe they never said it out loud, but I somehow knew that they believed that I would amount to something in the long haul. Without realizing it, that memory was my future.

As our children and grandkids grow, it's very important that we love and respect them from day one. An inherent part of that love is to believe in them — even in adolescence. Especially in adolescence! As our forebears encouraged us by saying "You have a promising future", we must always be on the lookout for the hopeful characteristics of all our children. No matter how far they may stray from our expected norms, we must continue to raise the signal of our faith in them. Our belief that they too will make it. No matter what else we leave them as legacy, our faith in them will be the most important key they will need to unlock the future.

It is the old Pygmalion principle that brought life to the breathless statue, and it continues to breathe life into every person who is loved for the promise they show, no matter how low they may be or feel. In the musical "My Fair Lady", Eliza Doolittle is transformed by the belief of Henry Higgins. In the down-trodden flower peddler of Convent Garden, he saw the promise of something more. He bet his life on that possibility he saw in her, and she won.

Pausing for a moment on the cusp of 2021, we just might realize that we are betwixt and between the expectations and promises that are driving forces from generation to generation. Susan Werner captures this idea in her haunting song "May I Suggest"… *There is a hope/ That's been expressed in you/ The hope of seven generations, maybe more/ And this is the faith/ That they invest in you/ It's that you'll do one better than was done before.* Meanwhile, Terry Tempest Williams expresses the notion that we must play the promise forward: *"The eyes of the future are looking back at us and they are praying for us to see beyond our own time. They are kneeling with clasped hands that we might act with restraint, leaving room for the life that is destined to come."*

We shall always be grateful for all those dear hearts and gentle people who raised us to do what's right for this world so that generations on their way will inherit our memory of their future. For instance, if we take seriously the issue of climate control, they just might inherit what's left of the promised land we call Earth.

1/3/2021

# Final Jeopardy

Over the past six months or so, we have endured a major pandemic that's killing us and an election that drove a divisive wedge between us. Beneath the surface another drama was unfolding that threatened to diminish us even further: the life-long host of "Jeopardy" was dying of cancer.

At the end of each weekday, when the sound and fury of nightly news programs concluded their chaotic reporting of the trauma and tragedy of the day, we welcomed the game show with host Alex Trebek. We watched the new contestants along with the returning champions compete with their knowledge of categories in Jeopardy and Double Jeopardy before Final Jeopardy produced a clear winner.

Contestants were given clues from which they were to answer by formulating the correct question. For example, the clue might be "Over 350,000 deaths due to Covid 19 have occurred in this country in the northern hemisphere in the last year". The answer would be "What is the United States"? Clue: "He was declared the winner of the presidential election." Answer: What is "It depends on if you choose truth or alternative facts"? Wrong! By the way, competent judges were on hand to disallow alternate facts as answers, which was a refreshing change from the White House news briefings.

Let's make sure we are on the same page with the very term before us. Merriam-Webster defines the "jeopardy" in two ways: "1 exposure to or imminence of death, loss, or injury: danger placing their lives in **jeopardy** workers in **jeopardy** of losing their jobs. 2 law: the danger that an accused person is subjected to when on trial for a criminal offense."

On Wednesday, when our nation's capital was attacked by domestic terrorists, law enforcement officers found themselves in jeopardy, their very lives on the line to defend the sanctuary of democracy. Senators and Representatives, who were carrying out their constitutional duty to certify the election results, were in jeopardy of losing their ability to execute their jobs. The anarchists who have been arrested for their heinous crimes are definitely in jail and in deep jeopardy. Even the current President, who clearly encouraged the insurrection, has put himself in jeopardy, even though he has several "get out of jail free" cards. Be that as it may, he is going to lose his job.

While I may not miss current occupant of the White House, I will miss Alex who has been a staple in our household for the past 37 years. He brought us the challenge of being informed in so many categories and challenged us to play the game along with the contestants with all our mind and heart and soul. He also came to each game with a dignity and touch of class that allowed us to trust and respect him for all he was worth. Those qualities filled a vacuum in the marketplace and body politic portrayed by the preceding newscasts on any given day.

As we move beyond January 20, our common hope is that we may return to the real priorities that are jeopardizing our country's future. Instead of attacking each other, we need to contain the pandemic with all the masks and distancing and vaccines we can throw at it. We have to face up to a failing economy, the racial unrest in the soul of this country, poverty and lack of health care... we know the list all too well because of what has not been done.

Final clue: "Name four things that might bring us together".
Final answer: "What are faith, hope, love, and the return of an older
game show called 'Truth or Consequences'"?

1/10/2021

# The Courage of Our Convictions

Call it what you will, but that violent insurrection against our country last week was nothing more than a mob scene gone berserk. They had been invited and incited by President Trump who tweeted to his base on December 19: "Big protest in D.C. on January 6th. Be there, will be wild!" "Wild" was an understatement. As I watched the madness, I was reminded of another mob that turned the tide in my life nearly sixty years earlier when one person's profile in courage made all the difference in the world.

In the long hot summer of 1964, my hometown had become one of the targets of the Freedom Summer project to encourage our African Americans to register to vote. Even though they represented nearly 70% of our town, they were disenfranchised from voting through many guises of voter suppression. This effort would eventually lead to the passage of the Civil Rights Act and the Voting Rights Act. All of this is set in what's famously known as the Old South, which had gone to war against the United States for the right to enslave other humans.

The fearsome "outside agitators" were mostly peaceful college students who were giving their summer in what they thought to be a patriotic cause for voting rights for all Americans. Most of the protestant churches in town began to gradually prohibit these white students from coming to worship, but the Presbyterians continued to welcome them, which did not set too well with the powers that be. On one Sunday, members of the White Citizens' Council formed a human fence around the Presbyterian Church, and I watched as they literally beat up those students who were innocently going to church.

Meanwhile, the young Presbyterian minister who was serving in his first parish, made a crucial decision that would change my life and the lives of others through his courage to stand up for what was right rather than give in to the demands of a fearful community. He came into the sanctuary and simply declared that he could not serve in a church that would not open its doors to anyone and everyone. And with that he resigned. Never mind that he was one of the brightest and best, graduating from Washington and Lee and Union Theological Seminary and was himself a native Mississippian. Never mind that his wife was pregnant with their fourth child. Never mind that he did not know the full implication of his action or where he might go next. Like Atticus Finch, Dick Harbison chose to confront this confederacy of complicity and to live by the courage of his convictions. For me, that courage and those convictions became a North Star that has helped me navigate the journey of a lifetime.

While that incident is old, it has guided me through many dangers, toils and snares. And while we may have come a very long way toward liberty and justice for all our citizens, there's a strange bitterness let loose in our land that wants us to go way back there to what truly were the dark days of our history. During my lifetime many things did change for the better. Or, so I thought, until I watched the mob of white Christian zealots wearing sweatshirts proclaiming "God, Guns, Trump" and carrying "Jesus is my savior; Trump is my president" flags that declared their crazy deities and illustrating that fools do indeed rush in where our better angels better not tread on the likes of them.

We dare not turn a deaf ear nor a blind eye to these awful shenanigans of treason and by our silence give any form of credence to such a shameful act. America deserves our courage to stop this madness.

1/17/2021

# Hoodwinked and Bamboozled

In an attempt to save face and cover his dismal inaugural exposure four years ago, the then newly elected President had to resort to a strategy that would beguile his next four years in office. The water hit the proverbial wheel on the first day in office when a dispute arose in the land as to just how many folks showed up for the inauguration. Looking at information provided by the National Park Service, the press approximated that there were about 160,000 odd people lining the mall. Rather than confuse the issue with such reliable data here, let's just say someone at the White House believed that this number was a crucial turning point in American history. A war on the news media — aka fake news — ensued, and a new political weapon was unleashed by some blonde with bad makeup: **"alternative facts"** — which could make the attendance any number you wanted it to be.

How well I remember being taught many alternative facts as a child of the old south: We actually won the war of northern aggression! The south will rise again. Black people are inferior, and they prefer segregation. You cannot legislate morality. Outside agitators are undermining wonderful God-given way of life.

During my freshman year in high school, this rather buxom woman wearing her DAR sash appeared on our stage during one assembly holding what seemed to be a children's book about rabbits. She was there to show us the naked truth that this book was produced by communists — "godless communists" — to undermine a well-known fact of southern history and kiddie lit: little black rabbits and little white rabbits never play together! Never! It was at that moment that I discovered this tiny gizmo in my gizzard: my crap detector went off.

**"An inconvenient truth"** was the phrase featured in Al Gore's 2006 documentary on global warming. It's a different nuance to "alternate facts". The truth of global warming is very verifiable, and the science was there to prove it. The problem was finding enough ears surrounding enough open minds to be convinced that this just might be the honest-to-God situation that would end the world, not with a bang but with the familiar and simple whimper: "I can't breathe". When Galileo discovered those other moons of Jupiter and exclaimed that this was indeed a solar-centric universe, the Church's reality was confronted with both alternative fact and inconvenient truth to its Aristotelian norms of God's creation which was turned upside down and inside out.

Lest we forget, when our white forebears thought they had discovered America, they coined the phrase "we hold these **truths to be self-evident**", and dared to proclaim that the first of these was that we are all "created equal". However, the DAR lady got on stage to declare that some of us were created more equal than others. And there were several inconvenient truths that hampered their early endeavors: certain indigenous people were already living on our land, and owning black lives mattered in establishing capitalism as the American economic principle, their equality, freedom and human dignity to the contrary notwithstanding.

Ever the politician, Governor Pontius Pilate knew how to stir up the mob with right wing religious zealots yelling "crucify him" ["Lock her up" would be an echo of the same mentality] and military tactical forces ready to kill another traitor other than Barabas who was guilty of insurrection. After his exasperating conversation with a would-be king of the Jews, Pilate washed his dirty hands of the whole mess with a sarcastic and rhetorical question, nullifying any answer: **"What is truth?"**

1/24/2021

# A Confederacy of Complicated Complicity

How in the world did my little hometown pull a reverse ratio in order to maintain what the citizens of white persuasion called keeping "a way of life" alive for several centuries? In the last half of the 20th Century, the "minority" of non-voting citizens was approximately 70%, who happened to be of the ineligible black persuasion.

You did not need a wall in those days to keep the lines of demarcation since the color of your skin – rather than the content of your character – was fairly indelible. Railroad tracks served as a mild steel barrier for housing and neighborhood distinction. Signs were also helpful for those who could read: Whites Only, Colored Only. As a child, I never was aware of the discrepancies that segregated little white boys like me from our majority of citizens other than thinking we were better off for some unknown reason.

Behind and beneath all of this blatant inequality, I must have wondered how in the world did this government of the people and by the people and for the people in my hometown get so catawampus from those founding principles of liberty and justice for all? The answer was as obvious as the white nose on my face and the black noses on theirs: that's just how it is and don't rock the boat. At least, that's how it was way back when.

Lo and behold, black history did matter just like each black life, and no matter how it was denied or debunked, it was as mainstream as the white counterpart. As children of this place and time, we were not taught to hate as much as we were encouraged to disregard those people and their unfortunate plight of being born black. Such disregard led to disrespect and apathy, which fostered a kind of white privilege we came to accept as our "way of life."

Thus developed a severe complicity among the white folks who were forced by their compatriots to swear an unsaid allegiance to keeping the things as they were. While the KKK had served as Christian terrorists to keep the peace in their own way, the White Citizens' Council went about with southern charm and genteel force to stop the effort to integrate schools and prevent blacks from daring to register to vote. Just about every white citizen and business establishment had to join ranks. I remember the Citizens Council decal on our front door.

These white citizens were part and parcel of the village that raised me and my peers. Like the wonderful characters in Thornton Wilder's *Our Town,* these were good people. Honorable white folk just trying their dead level best to do what they deemed right with the cards they had been dealt. That was also true of some of their southern ancestors who justified owning slaves as "a way of life". While some of these white citizens did let me down, others seem to shine some glimmer of light in the darkness of what was mildly called "race relations".

We have indeed come a long way since those not-so-long-ago days of yore, yet we still have miles to go before we can sleep in the peace that passes understanding just how we ever thought such things were a way of living. At the recent Inauguration, the youthful poet, Amanda Gorman, poignantly pointed us all in the right direction: *Scripture tells us to envision/ that everyone shall sit under their own vine and fig tree/ And no one shall make them afraid/ If we're to live up to our own time.../ It's because being*

*American is more than a pride we inherit, / it's the past we step into/ and how we repair it...*

1/31/2021

# Cold Wars and Warm Welcomes

While we never had to worry about insurrections insti-
gated by the president who clearly lost the election to take over
Washington and stop the democratic election process on which the
nation was founded, we had other important fish to fry to protect
our country in the days of my youth. Growing up southern was
not a piece of cake, and civic duty was always calling us to save our
town from enemies — both foreign and domestic. In the 1950's,
for example, in the prime of my teenage years, I would serve as a
capricious cadet on the local Civil Air Patrol to stand watch against
the invasion of Soviet aircraft. It was also a time when the sovereign
state of Mississippi, realizing that it might not have won the Civil
War, had launched a "be kind to Yankees" offensive.

As the Cold War heated up after Sputnik had been launched
into the heavens above us, people lived in the dreadful anticipation of an all-out nuclear war with the Ruskies. Folks in our town
started digging into their backyards and constructing bomb shelters against that dreaded day. They stocked canned goods and water
and ammunition enough for their own household, leaving the rest
of us as sitting targets.

Southern communities like ours formed Civil Air Patrols to
watch for that fearful moment when the enemy air force would be
invading our sacred southern air space. All hands were needed
to man the observation tower located just behind the library and
tennis courts. Before we climbed up the ladder into the wooden
tower, we had extensive training in identifying the USSR Migs
in order to distinguish them from the crop dusters that kept our
cotton free from boll weevils. I have no earthly idea how many

hours I stood guard, but at the end of my watch I was happy to report that not one Russian bomb was dropped on Canton.

While anticipating a cold war from some alien enemy half a world away, things were warming up from our "recent unpleasantness" with those people north of the Mason-Dixon. Rumor had it that if they would give us back our silver, we'd forget the whole thing. During Southern Hospitality Week, Yankees were intentionally targeted at our roadblock set just north of town on U.S. Highway 51, which ran from Lake Superior through Memphis to New Orleans. Boy Scout troops were pressed into active duty in this captivating enterprise. As south bound cars entered the boulevard into town, anyone from out of state would be flagged and in three blocks pulled to the side of the road by law enforcement officials who would invite them to the nearby faux antebellum hospitality booth where southern belles in hoop skirts would serve them refreshments. This charm offensive seemed to work, and no one ridiculed our dialects and drawls or the pulchritude of our Dixie darlings.

Somewhere between last month's open siege on our Capitol itself from the enemy within our borders and the welcoming comforts of down home hospitality, there's hope for ample grace to keep us alive long enough to pass the peace to a new generation of capricious teenagers who will search their skies for migrating Canadian geese rather than bombers and open their minds and hearts and voices with a great big "welcome y"all" that's wide enough to invite everybody into what President Reagan had called these United States in his farewell address: "the shining city upon a hill… open to any one with the will and the heart to get here."

2/7/2021

# Sabbath as a Sanctuary in Time

Coming on the last day or the first day of the week [depending on your religious upbringing], the Sabbath is a hinge that binds our days into a profane and holy history of many chapters. When I used to work for a living as a minister, I often referred to the "tyranny of the Sabbath" and meant by that the relentless march of time that demanded I be ready to lead worship and preach a sermon worthy of my hearers [often referred to as the preacher's one hour a week job]. In these more laidback wonder years of retirement, I've had a change of heart and mind that has led me to a new way of seeing the Sabbath — as more of a sanctuary within time itself.

Observing the Sabbath is the exhortation, the explanation, and the excuse for getting together on Sunday to worship or whatever else. Something greater happens than just "come to Jesus" or "personal salvation", or earning points with God by keeping this rather easy commandment. Simply being together is at the heart of it, along with the strange chemistry inherent in the mixture of sacred and secular. Where else in our culture do sound people come together to sing songs in harmony with an organ? Or sit in pews and pray together? And you know what happens? It dawns on us that we are drawn here by a hankering to belong. We belong with each other in the "beloved community". We belong to a God who covenanted with us way back in Exodus 20.

There are times in our lives when we find it hard to do Sundays. When we've lost faith in ourselves or the church or even in God. The good news is that the covenant community is able to keep our faith going even when we seemed to have lost our faith to go on. Even when we can't make church on Sunday, our friends and neighbors — who "share our mutual woes, our mutual burdens bear and often for each other flows the sympathizing tear" — are there in our stead holding steady on theirs and all our promises to be Church. Our church family will keep the sabbath for us and remember us. Even when a pandemic forces us to close the doors for months of Sundays.

That famous bar in Boston called "Cheers" had a theme song that could double as a choral call to worship: *Making your way in the world today/ Takes everything you've got/ Taking a break from all your worries/ Sure would help a lot/ Wouldn't you like to get away?/ Sometimes you want to go/ Where everybody knows your name/ And they're always glad you came/ You want to be where you can see/ Our troubles are all the same/ You want to be where everybody knows your name.* On any day of the week, that is indeed a sanctuary in time that so many of us long for in order to feel right at home with each other.

"Out of all the gin joints in all the towns in all the world" was Bogie's way of describing another bar in Casablanca, with an appropriate song for this Valentine's Day. It captures the same depth of intimacy that God's covenant of love asks that we remember those fundamental things that apply, especially on Sunday mornings like this one: *You must remember this/ a kiss is just a kiss/ a sigh is just a sigh/ the fundamental things apply/ as time goes by.* We'll always have the Sabbath. And each other.

2/14/2021

# When One Cheer Is Enough

The University of Mississippi in Oxford has many claims to fame, but it's graduates will tell you that the best one is the famous cheer that is exclaimed with pride, joy and a twist of irony: *Hotty toddy/ Gosh almighty/ who in the hell are we? Hey!/ Flim Flam, Bim Bam,/ Ole Miss, by damn!* While no one can tell you the deeper meanings of this yell, the cheer was a caustic affront to athletic foes and to the Southern Baptist Convention where curse words like "hell" and "damn" were considered an abomination unto the Lord. No one can explain "flim flam" and "bim bam". Besides, who needs three cheers when one hotty toddy will do?

When I was an innocent adolescent, football was king of all sports for southern boys. I started playing when I was seven and did not quit until I was eighteen. In the early 1950s, we could only listen to the Ole Miss games on the radio and imagine the running backs and tight ends and quarterbacks doing their darndest to beat the other team. We'd tune into announcer Bill Goodrich and hear him utter his famous "Whew-hoo, mercy!" at the end of outstanding plays.

Before you could say "hotty toddy", television crept into our homes. The first television broadcast I ever watched was the Sugar Bowl from Tulane stadium in New Orleans. Since Mississippi did not have any television stations, we drove all the way to Memphis to watch it on Uncle Paul's brand new TV set as Georgia Tech soundly defeated Ole Miss. [Uncle Paul Dorman, by the way, was a news anchor in Memphis on station WREC, from high atop the Peabody Hotel. He had the right stuff that enabled him to move from radio to television during those awkward transitions.]

Once that new media cat was out of the bag, and televisions made the world fit into little black and white screens in our dens, Katy could no longer bar the door. Football, for example, became much larger than the Southeastern Conference. We could watch UCLA or Ohio State in the Rose Bowl after the ladies were enthralled by the floral parade through Pasadena. Then we moved to the NFL and watched the professionals who could earn gazillions of dollars and make me wonder why I quit football when I was eighteen.

When you think about the transformative power of television in our lives over the past seven decades or so, you don't know whether to cheer or not. It has had some very positive effects and brought our world together in awe of things like landing on the moon. We'd watch Walter Cronkite tell us the news from around the globe and know "that's the way it was". We were shocked by the horrors of racism as we watched police dogs attack African Americans in neighboring Alabama. The aftershock made its way to Congress, and the Civil Rights Act of 1964 became law enough to grant all our citizens all the rights they deserve.

Last month, our smart televisions invaded our homes with their telecast of homegrown terrorism as a mob of white supremacists plundered our Capitol and threatened to kill our legislatures after their cheerleader-in-chief pointed toward the enemy and urged them to "Fight like hell!" And, if you'll pardon my Southeastern Conference vernacular, "by damn" if they didn't do exactly as they were told. Armed to the hilt with Rebel flags and lynching nooses, all hell broke loose and spilled those ungodly but undeniable images into our American memory and collective conscience.

2/21/2021

# Rebels With a Cause

In the autumn of 1962, the Ole Miss "Rebels" [former politically incorrect nickname] football team was on its way to an undefeated season and capturing the national championship without the benefit of their own campus stadium. It was being occupied by federal troops who were there to make sure that James Meredith, the first African American student, could attend classes. All kinds of chaos surrounded his admission, beginning earlier in the state Capitol.

As a member of the Fourth Estate for my college newspaper, I had a press pass that got me admitted to the notable incident that took place in the Office of Education within the State Building in Jackson. Governor Ross Barnett had unlawfully declared himself the Registrar for the University and set up the confrontation for Meredith to register for admission through him. The press was gathered in the hallway leading to the office where the Governor stood in the doorway. Accompanied by two tall white guards from the U.S. Justice Department, the applicant approaches the Governor/Registar who inquires "Which one of you gentlemen is Mr. Meredith?" When the laughter subsided, the whole incident was redone on a more serious level to benefit the television cameras trying to capture the gravity of the moment.

Short of statue to begin with, James Meredith was the only black guy within miles. Ross Barnett was rather rotund and blustery and, some would argue, politically challenged. His gubernatorial campaign jingle was "Roll With Ross", and his bumper sticker word was "Never!". Everybody knew what that meant. Several weeks later he would appear at the Ole Miss and Houston football game at Memorial Stadium in Jackson and give his three-sentence speech over and over again in proper southern drawl: "I looove Mississippi. I looove her people. I looove and respect our heritage." The crowd roared between each phrase, and we all knew it had something to do with "Never!"

On the night of September 30, 1962, riots broke out on the University campus in Oxford, and the young Episcopal chaplain, Duncan Gray Jr., stood his ground right in the middle of the melee in trying to quell and calm the students involved. Duncan's father became the Bishop of the Mississippi Diocese, as did Duncan and his son after him. The best portrait of him was a book by Baptist preacher, Will Campbell, entitled And Also with You: Duncan Gray and the American Dilemma.

Every other chapter juxtaposes the life of Duncan Gray, Jr. and the Mississippi Greys, that group of Ole Miss students who fought to defend the Lost Cause of the Confederacy until all of them had given the last full measure of their devotion at the Battle of Gettysburg. Campbell wanted us to see that the passions that drove them were part and parcel of Duncan's passions for racial justice. The temperaments of the rioters on campus that autumn evening were also part of the same cloth.

The campus rebellion would be quelled. "Never!" would eventually yield to "Well, maybe." Ross Barnett would end up in lower parts of Neverland. James Meredith would graduate from Ole Miss. Duncan would become the Bishop of Mississippi Episcopalians and Chancellor of the University of the South in Sewanee, Tennessee.

When Will Campbell was writing his book, he stayed in the Sewanee Inn and interviewed the proprietor who had been there for years to get the lowdown on Bishop Gray. Her answer was the best line in the book: "Duncan Gray was the only man I've ever met who wasn't up to something." Blessed are the unassuming for they shall become those peacemakers who show us we are all children of God.

2/28/2021

# The Unseemly Demise of My Sister's Cat

While there's very little glory in the gory details of this sordid tale that ends in *cat*astrophe, my conscience continues to plague me until I have let most of the known world know what happened on that bloody day. I'm not big on confession [even during Lent], but I'm scared that purgatory and/or hell itself will literally have kitty litter all over the place. And no more *cat*naps!

On good days, I am indifferent towards most cats because a childhood experience when I was traumatized by several domestic feline terrorist on the overloaded dining room table of an elderly relative's Sunday dinner. These untoward creatures would saunter silently amid the platters and plates filled with southern culinary delights and stare at me in particular. My appetite left the room, and I soon followed.

Fast forward to my final years at college when I made a dash home in my car to collect a few things I had forgotten on my most recent trip. It was mid-morning, and no one was at home. My parents were at work and my twelve-year younger sister, Katherine, was at school.

Rather than dawdle or dilly-dally, I threw my stuff in the car and began backing out the driveway...until I felt a thud under my wheel. Looking under the car, I discovered to my dismay that Katherine's white cat had accidently crawled under the car and was now squashed, it's white fur red with blood. I knew that she loved this cat and would be wrought with despair were I to leave it there for her to discover that an accident of unknown origin had taken all the lives left for this poor puss. Best to remove the evidence.

I grabbed a shovel and placed the deceased animal in a brown paper grocery bag and carried it to a nearby town creek for disposal, if not a proper burial. I let the cat out of the bag to flow freely and graciously into some murky oblivion down the creek. But I got left holding the bag of remorse and wondering what I might do for recompense and restitution for such a heinous crime of slaughtering my sister's helpless white cat.

Unaccustomed to such a plight, I drove to the local veterinary office where our family friend O'dell Foster served a nurse. She would understand. She could help me undo this dastardly deed, even though the cat was at fault. After confessing to the crime, I asked if she might know where I could find a cat of the same ilk to replace the flat cat in the driveway. She tried to dissuade me from such a course of action, claiming that cats are particular, peculiar and irreplaceable. A cat is a cat I reasoned, and a live one is better than a dead one. And they happened to have a white one of similar vintage and proportion. Who would ever know?

The new white cat and I hauled tail back to the house before anyone had returned, and I left that replacement in mint condition on the back porch before heading back to college justified and off the hook. And I would certainly hope that my sister would have the common decency to not call the new cat by the former cat's name: Pancake!

A postscript for this story. In her earlier childhood, Katherine had received two little ducklings for Easter. They would eventually grow into her beloved pet ducks until they got run over taking their ever-loving time crossing the street. Their names were Dilly and Dally.

3/7/2021

# Good Ancestors Are Hard to Find

As an amateur dabbler in matters of my family tree, I try to keep it fertilized and trim it occasionally when it promises bad fruit or withered limbs. I do hit a snag as to whether certain ancestors might not be kith and kin and would wish I had some choice in picking a more nobler pedigree. Cassius reminded us and his friend that "The fault, dear Brutus, is not in our stars / But in ourselves, that we are underlings". Stumbling around in our own stash of stardust, we don't get to choose our ancestors who, over generations, created the likes of us in their images and with their sordid baggage.

As St. Patrick's Day looms largely on this week's horizon, I'd like to thank my lucky stars that I have quite a bit of Irish in my DNA. When I hear the sordid stories of how the Irish immigrants were treated upon their arrival to this country in the nineteenth century, I am proud of my great grandmother's people who came through Canada to arrive in northern Michigan's copper mining country. And "while the Irish need not apply" might have been the watchword in other parts of this emerging nation, they let my great grandfather be a smelter in the Calumet copper mine near Lake Superior.

From Scotland, another great grandfather set sail to start a new life in Chicago, where he was a tailor of men's clothing. His son would become a telegrapher for the Illinois Central Railroad and end up in the middle of Mississippi on the main line between Chicago and New Orleans. And that's where he met my Michigan grandmother to create the family tree containing the Crawford branch. With all these geographical and genetical backgrounds,

I feel like I'm a half-breed like Jesus. While the Bible is careful to point out that Joseph was of the "house and lineage of David", his name was not on the birth certificate.

This would be the proper place to drop some jaw-gaping names from up in those higher branches, but I don't think that Uncle William [the Conqueror] would want me to give away too many family secrets beyond the Bayeux Tapestry's story of his overwhelming the Brits at Hastings. So, let's just assume that your people are just like my people; they don't actually grow on trees like money. They are created in a more loving way and spend their lives procreating their descendants and have to take what they get which happens to be the likes of us.

While I don't play golf nor wear a kilt, I'll raise a wee dram on St. Patty's Day to recall and reclaim my Scotch Irish heritage. At the same time, I need to let the next generation know about their claims to fame just might have more to do with inherited values than the stock from which we came. More about the content of our character than any colors of our skins, like poor little blue-blooded Archie.

Maybe it is in our stars after all, or the stardust in us all. We are "carbon" copies of each other and cloned in the spitting image of a Creator who gives us the gift of life itself and simply ask that we try to be the best ancestors in the world for the whole blooming human family. And, as our brother Jesus would put it, color of your skin or country of origin or gender or creed to the contrary notwithstanding.

3/14/2021

# Thank God for Good Government

While affirming the separation of church and state, I thank God for giving us governments by which we may live together for the common good. From the federal to the local levels, governments made me into the person writing these words that public schools taught me to use. Government protected me from diseases and disasters and enemies, foreign and domestic. From Medicare to Social Security, it has been the helping hand for us older folk. All the roads I have travelled in my lifetime were built by the governments of the people and by the people and for the people. One road project in particular hit close to home, literally and figuratively.

When Dwight Eisenhower was our President, he led us into infrastructure endeavors that strengthened our economy as never before, and the Interstate Highway System was one of the most important and enduring. This particular highway bill was ratified and signed in 1956 as a means of defending our major cities in case of a nuclear attack. The project was going strong when I graduated from high school in 1960 and paved the way for me to become old enough to realize how good government makes for a great place in which to live.

 Fate played an important role in a series of circumstances that led me to building Interstate Highway 55 between Memphis and New Orleans. My steady girlfriend in my senior year of high school happened to be the daughter of the major contractor for the Interstate project in the area. He graciously hired me to work for the four summers of my college years.

In the first summer I worked as a "grease monkey" servicing the earth-moving machines and in charge of the generators that produced the lighting for the night crew. Over the four summers I learned to operate most of the Caterpillar equipment, and by my last summer, I was put in charge of a crew to build a small county road. The job educated me to see the values of hard work and to appreciate all the other people involved in this project. It "literally" educated me with making enough money to totally pay for all my college costs.

So, you can see why I thank God for government, from Eisenhower on. It is the infrastructure that creates the infrastructure whereby we all prosper and grow. Without it, how would you ever get to work without the roads or provide for the Covid 19 vaccines? So I have a hard time when I hear people complaining about too much government when so much of my life is the beneficiary of good government.

Our friend from several Chautauqua summers is the talented and passionate pastor of the Ebenezer Baptist Church in Atlanta who recently became the Senator from Georgia. This past week, Rev. Raphael Warnock made his first address on the floor of the senate supporting the Voting Rights Bill and received a standing ovation. At one point he said, *"As a man of faith, I believe democracy is the political enactment of a spiritual idea: the sacred worth of all human beings."*

Thank God those anarchists who tried to do us in on January 6, failed to "stop the count" of votes, but their ugly legacy lingers. Good government prevailed against that fratricidal tyranny, but we still have a long and winding road to travel in order to build that highway Isaiah imagined: *In the wilderness prepare the way*

*of the Lord, make straight in the desert a highway for our God...*
*Then the glory of the Lord shall be revealed, and all people shall see*
*it together.*

3/21/2021

# The Everlasting Last Supper

The original is a huge mural painted into the stucco on the refectory wall in an out-of-the-way convent called Santa Maria delle Grazie in Milan. We made a point to go out there one day to see the weathered version of Leonardo Da Vinci's treasured artwork just prior to its latest restoration. Far from being a museum or art gallery, the venue had just a few visitors allowing us space and time to observe the painting. I was somewhat taken aback by the fact that it was located in what Presbyterians would refer to as the fellowship hall just above the door leading to the kitchen. Since that first encounter with this all-too famous and familiar masterpiece, I have been plagued by its presence in all sorts of settings and situations.

Many years later, we wandered into the beautiful cathedral in Cusco, Peru, and saw yet another version with a lot of interesting details to distinguish it from a European last supper. Probably the most notable difference is that the meal's main dish is cuy — the Peruvian delicacy of guinea pig! Also, Jesus and his disciples are drinking chicha, which is a traditional Peruvian corn drink. It is believed that the artist painted Judas, the disciple who betrayed Jesus, to bear a resemblance to Francisco Pizarro, the Spanish conquistador responsible for the fall of the Inca empire!

When I arrived at the West End parish, the last thing on my mind was the Last Supper. This little "church in the wildwood" had served the small congregation for three-fourths of a century and was quite quaint in most of its decorum with the exception of a tacky paint-by-number rendition of the Leonardo's epic work hanging over the mantle in the women's parlor. Early on, in order to attract new members who might have artistic sensitivities, I quietly removed this lackluster reproduction and hid it in a closet. To my chagrin, the painting reappeared, as it would following other attempts to rid us of this Supper at Last by hiding it in a variety of places. Then, like some haunted miracle or bad penny, it would find its nail over the mantle. In short order, the parable of the paranoid pastor and his painting became common knowledge among some of the flock. A West End underground Da Vinci code group emerged with the primary goal of nabbing the culprit who kept bringing it back.

As a Presbyterian pastor I had to mind my P's & Q's when it came to observing the Holy Communion. In the early days a large tablecloth covered the elements, mainly to keep the flies away before the ceremony started. We then moved from serving the seated congregants with those tiny shot glasses in a round tray to intinction, inviting the participants to come forward to receive the elements. We also moved from "adults only" to letting the kids take the elements even though some adults argued that they wouldn't understand. On Christmas Eve, each row would come down and sit on the first pew to be personally served by the minister and always with an Elder as specified by the Book of Order, or I could have ended up in hell. That's where I heard one of the best responses to the Last Supper that came from a preschooler when I was saying — while serving — "This is the body and blood of Christ". She exclaimed "Yuck!" Who said kids don't get it?

After the supper, Jesus said unto them, "If you want to be in the picture, get on this side of the table."

3/28/2021

# The Grace of Easter's Enigma

Years ago, when I was her minister, the mother of a four-year-old confronted me with a profound question. While she and her son were dragging out the plastic eggs and stuffed bunnies in preparation for the upcoming Easter festivities, she realized that somehow this was a cultural trick and treat game for the spring. You sort of trick the kids into believing in miracles [rabbits laying eggs] and treat them with candy and new clothes. She suddenly felt a compulsion to teach her son about the true meaning of Easter. But she was stumped. How do you explain the enigma of Easter to your child, when you really don't understand it yourself? Check with your minister, of course!

I disappointed her with a dumbfounded look. If I had THE answer to that one, I'd be selling books or preaching on television. I hate to say "I don't know". I feel like I should invent something to prevent myself from coming over like a stick in the mud. But that's what I am: stuck in the same mud of obscurity as you when it comes to the mysteries of our faith. Especially when it comes to that greatest of all murder mysteries with the disappearing corpse. Easter is the darndest thing to figure, much less explain to a four-year-old. It scares us out of our wits like that angel in the graveyard asking those faithful women that first Easter sunrise, "Why are you looking for the living among the dead?"

Why do we have to understand everything? Or explain everything to our children to wipe away some of their wonder? Our reason for trying to understand the death and resurrection of Jesus is to gain some sense of control of the situation. To figure it out, or to use a word that's quite in vogue in church circles, to "discern" the real meaning of Easter for our own security in life. We sink or swim by such self-sufficiency. When Archimedes jumped in the bathtub and displaced water, he figured out how specific gravity made certain things float and others sink. "Eureka, I have it!" became the cry heard round the world.

Resurrection is beyond explanation and defies human logic. It simply flies in the face of all reality. But so does God's grace. And love. Try telling your child the real meaning of love. Or try explaining birth or death. But there's a catch, you see, which you really don't see. Can't see. When you come to the end of this blind alley, you discover it's a dead end, which is what life becomes without Easter.

I find it well-nigh to impossible to believe in Easter because it is such a scandal. Ridiculous. Incredible. There's no way on earth to explain someone rising from the dead — neither the whys nor the wherefores. Like the undeserved grace of God -- it simply happens, and we are struck deaf and dumb by all its intensity and insanity. We don't understand it. We can't control it. We don't deserve it. But it is freely given. When Christ left that tomb, something beyond reason came chasing us. Death defying love that now defines our living and throws light against all the shadows of our doubts. Eureka!

4/4/2021

# The Miracle of Easter Egg Leftovers

Back in olden days, the Easter bunny didn't know how to lay plastic eggs. She [assumed pronoun] produced the hard-boiled, dyed, and colorful real things to hide in obscure places for kids to find on the annual "hunt". Those adventurous searches for Easter eggs were quite daunting at times. When the game ended, the winner had the most eggs in her or his baskets. A few eggs were never found for many days, maybe even weeks. By then, however, they were easy to locate because of the stench that led you to find these Easter leftovers.

Even before the putrid smell of decaying eggs in your yard got your attention, there was something rotten about the whole Easter egg enterprise. I vividly recall one hunt when the youth group was in charge of running the show, which entailed procuring and hiding the eggs and refereeing the Easter morning event with the kids of the church. The children of assorted ages gathered on the front steps of the church awaiting the signal to begin the mad dashes throughout a prescribed area with an unspoken imperative to get as many as you can before someone else got there ahead of you.

Jordy was the youngest and smallest hunter who inadvertently got a late start. As the bigger egg chasers were stuffing their baskets and bringing the melee to an apparent finale, Jordy's basket was empty, and his countenance was extremely woeful and dismayed. Assessing the situation as unjust and beyond the pail of Christian charity, I called together a couple of youth sponsors and urged them to rectify our problem. Meanwhile, I took Jordy on a spin around the building and returned to the scene of the earlier crime where he happened to discover four rather obviously placed eggs.

As the two of us made our way back to the other hunters who were counting their bountiful loot, Jordy took my hand and stopped me in my tracks. In awe, he held up his little basket with four eggs and exclaimed: "It's a miracle!"

We seem to have forgotten that lesson we learned in kindergarten...that one about sharing. It is quite obvious that the disparity between the haves and the have-nots, both nationally and globally, has been growing exponentially over the past few decades and torn the fabric of our *E Pluribus Unum*. Those who seem to have their baskets full don't really give a rip about those without an egg to their name. They have learned to live with lavish lifestyles as if the game of life is defined by the Easter-egg-hunt aspiration and assumption that those who end up with the most wealth or whatever, win.

Operating from a perspective of limited scarcity, we just don't see the surplus of common wealth beyond belief. Consequently, we are selfishly headed for our tombs with all our eggs in the wrong baskets. Or, to paraphrase Jesus right after he pulled a reverse-Jordy miracle to feed five thousand people with a little boy's two fish and five loaves, "...where's the profit if you gain the whole world and lose your soul?" By the time the crowd had eaten the kid's fish and bread, the disciples collected twelve Easter baskets full of leftovers.

Other than when Jesus said that "unless we become like children" we don't have a snowball's chance in hell of seeing the kingdom of heaven, do you see what Jordy had in common with Him? They both epitomized what would become the watchword of this *Stumbling Over Stardust* blogging endeavor: "With all respect to heaven, the scene of the miracle is here, among us."

4/11/2021

# Discerners or Doers of the Word?

Every now and then a certain word will crop up in ecclesiastical jargon that will outdo its usefulness and should be retired. I recall in the 90's when church leaders were seeking the "cutting edge" of anything that might have enough hutzpah to coax a few new members into the fold. I was sitting next to an elderly friend at a Synod meeting where "cutting edge" was the clarion call for whatever when my friend nudged me and whispered, "the cutting edge for the church should be gerontology." After a few years of overuse, the cutting-edge syndrome became excruciatingly dull and useless.

The less cutting-edge word that has emerged in the past few years is "discerning", as in "discerning God's will". I can't figure out the origin of that word, but disciples of all stripes are overusing it as if Christendom itself will fall if not engaged in discerning something all the time. I have finally figured out that the word is a metaphorical filibuster for not deciding right now what God has in mind for us, which I find a bit off-putting since it's as clear as the day is long what God wants of us.

Early in my career as a resident theologian, my job was to explain God to the folk in the flock who were yearning to discern the same. Rev. Will Campbell showed up at my office one day, wanting to know how things were going. "Not too well, Campbell. I am giving it all I've got to reconcile the races here in the early 70's in middle of Mississippi." He then went on to explain to me that it was not my job to reconcile the races; God had done that, and my job was to make the announcement. No need to discern anymore or argue with that.

Rev. Campbell was asked by the University of Florida to participate in a debate on the death penalty. The person in favor of the penalty took his allotted time explaining why he thought state-sponsored killing was OK. Will got up and simply said he was against the death penalty because he thought it was tacky and sat down. The leader asked if he'd like to explain his answer, he replied that people could look up "tacky" in their dictionary: *not having or exhibiting good taste: marked by lack of style...*

In our everlasting debate about gun control in this country, Christians are up in arms trying to discern God's will on this issue. Rather than argue which gun Jesus would have used to defend himself and his disciples to prevent his crucifixion, what if we recalled God's commandment about not killing each other in the first place? When Jesus taught us all to love our neighbors, a certain lawyer asked a very persnickety question: "Well, Jesus, just who is my neighbor?" Hearing an undertone of sarcasm in the question, Jesus used a simple story to make his point that someone outside the faith [a Samaritan] saw the need and did the deed." Which of these three was the neighbor?" Jesus asked the deceptively discerning lawyer.

"The one who showed mercy," was his only and obvious reply.

"Bingo! You have discerned rightly, but now you must go and do likewise." Otherwise, it would be tacky to have been a discerning disciple who didn't do "diddly-squat" — there's a cutting-edge term for the church to mull [*to consider at length; ponder*]. Or how about "fish or cut bait" for Heaven's sake?

4/18/2021

# A Little More Breathing Room

The eyes and ears — along with the hearts and minds — of the whole world have been focussed on the trial of George Floyd until the jury's verdict was finally rendered on Monday, and we could all breathe a sigh of relief that some sort of dramatic change was in the air at last. When the truth of what happened was captured on a video by a young bystander, all other arguments to the contrary not withstanding were emptied of any meaning. In horror and dismay we all watched the white knee on the black neck and heard the haunting words "I can't breathe."

Killing another human being is heinous enough and the lowest common denominator under any circumstance, no matter for what reason or how it is executed. Of course, guns tend to be the most convenient choice these days. Living in a country like this where getting a gun is seen as a "God-given right" is equivalent to blaming God for anything that one does with all those guns. Just think of the mass shootings that have taken place since the beginning of this year, never mind that a total of 13,361 Americans have been killed by guns since this year began. Talk about an outrageous pandemic!

Rather than waste a bullet, the guilty officer knelt on the neck of the victim for well nigh unto ten long minutes, and he did so with outrageous indignation and obvious nonchalance toward the handcuffed and subdued Mr. Floyd. Someone has argued that the callous death had nothing to do with the failure of the victim's heart but with the hardness of that officer's heart. What we all saw that fateful day was self-evident truth about systemic racism that must be rooted out of our culture in order for all of us to have a little more breathing room for getting along better with our neighbors.

Between the masks and distancing of Covid19 and the painfully divisive politics of 2020, some of us found it emotionally and spiritually claustrophobic. And don't forget that inconvenient truth of climate deterioration which will surely take our breath away. No matter what side you might be on in the great divide that was intentionally created by the last administration to foster that conflict and chaos we witnessed on January 6, we must overcome all our differences in order to go forward with liberty and justice for all of us. George Floyd's unjustified death will not have been in vain if we all see it as a chance for a new birth of freedom once again.

This could be our balm in Gilead "that makes the wounded whole...that calms the sin-sick soul" of our beloved country. In his collection of meditations entitled The Magnificent Defeat, Frederick Buechner says it so well: *Heaven knows terrible things happen to people in this world. The good die young, and the wicked prosper, and in any one town, anywhere, there is grief enough to freeze the blood. But from deep within whatever the hidden spring is that life wells up from, there wells up into our lives, even at their darkest and maybe especially then, a power to heal, to breathe new life into us.*

4/25/2021

# Being Dead Is No Excuse

Today's catchy yet mysterious title is borrowed from a classic book by the same name on how grief and grace use groceries to enable those of us left behind after the funeral to manage our survival with some solace and soul food. The two southern ladies who wrote the charming culinary guide try to convince the readers that *Folks in the Delta have a strong sense of community, and being dead is no impediment to belonging to it. Down South, they don't forget you when you've up and died–in fact, they visit you more often. But there are quintessential rules and rituals for kicking the bucket tastefully. Having a flawless funeral is one of them.*

Here's a snippet: *After the solemnity of the church service and finality of the grave, the people of the Mississippi Delta are just dying to get to the house of the bereaved for the reception. This is one of the three times a Southerner gets out all the good china and silver; the other two are christenings and weddings. The silver has most likely been specially polished for the occasion. Polishing silver is the Southern lady's version of grief therapy.*

While the two authors take delightful liberties to make this enterprise part of the southern culture, my experience with other people, up to and including Yankees, has led me to believe that this is a universal truth: funeral food is not just a southern thing. When death occurs within any community, there's this groundswell of grief which leads to an outpouring of a bountiful buffet upon the immediate family of the deceased.

Ladies of the kitchen suddenly appear and make themselves at home. Chicken and broccoli casseroles are placed in ovens for heating. Neatly trimmed sandwiches covered in cellophane are brought in by the neighbors. Delicious cakes adorn beautiful plates which always have a piece of masking tape on the bottom bearing the name of the cook. After the funeral itself, the folding tables covered with the finest linen in the fellowship hall hardly have enough space for another dish of those little barbecue smoke sausages. Have you ever wondered why in the world the living mourn the dead around a dining room table loaded with enough food to feed Coxey's Army?

Maybe all this food is more for the soul than the body — both for the donor and those for whom it is cooked. It's how culinary craft is utilized to express in deed what they cannot say in word. It's a tasty and tangible way of expressing the sacrament of sorrow that binds the living together in the reality of death. And when the service and the accompanying meal are over and the house finally left to those who inhabit it, tears emerge as they look under the plates at the names written on masking tape; gracious cooks who brought their special offering to the altar of mutual sadness.

The origin of such a custom is beyond me, but we have a tradition in the church that's very much like it. Even though he never had a proper southern funeral, we still remember the death of Jesus, and his followers still gather at a table furnished with the gift of groceries — some bread and a little wine. These elements speak beyond our hunger for bread alone, and our cups overflow as we remember the gift of amazing grace. And if you look closely enough, you can see his initials taped beneath the cup.

5/2/2021

# Motherless Children of Another Exodus

The second chapter of Exodus begins with a story of a mother's sleuth and chicanery to outwit the Pharaoh's command that all the boys born to the Israelite slaves by killed. This unsung lady hid her little newborn in a basket in the bulrushes on the Nile in Egypt where the Pharaoh's daughter discovers him, takes him home and unwittingly hires his birth mother as the nursemaid. She names the kid Moses because, as she put it, "I drew him out of the water."

Even with a such a confusing family tree, Moses emerges as the biblical hero who will confront the evil regime in Egypt and demand that his people [who just happen to be God's people] be given walking papers so that they can set out on the Exodus toward some land deal that God kept promising. The long road from slavery to that land of milk and honey [but no oil] took the better part of forty years. Moses never put foot in it and knew not the mother who had to give him up in order to bless him on his way to Mt. Sinai's Torah that said "Honor your mother…, that your days may be long in the land that the Lord your God is giving you." Now, there's the possibility of a great plot for a movie starring the NRA's late Charlton Heston.

Mother's Day just might be a good time for us to focus our attention on the mothers of a current exodus from Central America and Mexico who have to put their sons and daughters in the stream of migrants seeking safety from all sorts of Pharaohs trying to kill them. Some of them actually end up in the Rio Grande River, just like Moses. However, too many of us are in "denial" about what's happening to these borderline children who are getting the short end of an ugly stick. If you listen carefully, you can almost hear the mothers just south of our border weeping for their children [who just happen to be God's children]. Just like that weeping sound out of Ramah that Jeremiah recalls: the wailing of Rachel [wife of Jacob and mother of Joseph and Benjamin] as her children are being led **into** Egyptian captivity and slavery right over her grave.

In 1870, Julia Ward Howe was one of the first Americans to intimate the idea of a day to honor mothers. She was an abolitionist, served as a nurse in the Civil War, and wrote "The Battle Hymn of the Republic." She also wrote these words for a Mother's Day proclamation: *Arise, then...women of this day! Whether our baptism be that of water or of tears! Say firmly: Our sons shall not be taken from us to unlearn all that we have been able to teach them of charity, mercy and patience. We, women of one country, will be too tender of those of another country to allow our sons to be trained to injure theirs.*

Mothers without borders or boundaries can become a strong force for peace and non-violence which might threaten the unjust powers in our day and time. In her column last week, Margaret Renkl from Nashville, asks us to look at Mother's Day differently: *Mother's Day is a saccharine invention, a national fairy tale in a nation that does almost nothing to support mothers. But it is also a day for contemplating the ways in which we're connected to one another, through times of joy and times of sorrow, across time and across species.*

5/9/2021

# The Right to Bare Arms

The early part of 2021 witnessed the rollout of Covid 19 vaccines, and I was glad to be in that number of persons vaccinated by the middle of February. And the march goes on as we wait for all of us to get those shots. We were asked to bare our arms as a patriotic and medical duty to slow down this unseen pandemic that's killing us.

Speaking of killings, one wonders where the NRA has been lately. We have had ten mass shootings per week so far this year; 194 in all. [A mass shooting is when four or more people are killed or wounded] Since the pandemic has risen to the top of heap as the reason for most deaths in this country, mass shootings have taken a hit and are having to bite their own bullets. By the middle of May, 15,439 Americans have been killed so far this year by gun violence.

Gun violence started with a bang this past January 6, in the attack on our own Capitol by our own gun-toting citizenry. Explain that to your seven-year-old or teach that to your high school civics class. As I watched this horror unfurl like some flag with the leader of the insurgency's name emboldened on it, I recalled other terrible incidents in our nation's recent history like the assignations of President Kennedy and Rev. Martin Luther King, Jr. Visions of 9/11 came of the screen of my memory but there was a stark difference in that the enemy came from beyond us. Now the enemy is within the wall we were building to keep out other hoodlums. Where was the House Un-American Activity Committee when we needed them most?

 The crowd was composed of white supremacists' gangs dressed in military garb rather than white robes and hoods. The vigilante take over was full of flapping flags including several Rebel ones representing another lost cause when well-meaning southerners attempted to take over our nation in defense of slavery. Most of the flags this January had the Agitator-in-Chief's name on them. I saw one flag declaring that "Jesus is my savior" and "Trump is my president." I wondered who would save Jesus from his association with this bunch of hell raisers. When he was born in Bethlehem, another anarchist ruler, King Herod, went berserk and had all the baby boys slaughtered to assuage any fears of his own loss of power. He [like our former president] would not be a loser, especially to some kid born in a barn. The only flag that ever flew over Jesus was the makeshift one nailed to his cross: "King of the Jews".

Baring our naked arms for a vaccine, wearing a mask, and keeping our distance, and washing our hands were and are things that are easy enough and patriotic in that we help prevent the spread of Covid 19 to the helpless among us. We shorten the time to return to normalcy with everything reopening. When it comes to bearing the truth, that's a different story altogether. We have learned to live with alternate facts and legends composed of lies that fit our own fancies and fantasies: the election was stolen; owning more ammo than we need and bigger guns than our neighbors is our God-given right; those were just "tourist and visitors" who invaded the Capitol on January 6, according to the remake of that historical event we all witnessed. Or were we just being hoodwinked by fake news?

5/16/2021

# You Ring; We Bring

Adjusting to special circumstance of Covid 19, grocery stores began offering a delivery service to facilitate shoppers from having to enter the premises. This is not a new concept, but a welcomed one to those unable to get to the store. In my long-past youth, I worked for a local grocery whose niche was declared by its slogan: "May's Food Market: You Ring; We Bring".

I must have been all of thirteen when I showed up at six o'clock for that first Saturday as a bag boy who would eventually end up being a gregarious grocer with a variety of skills culminating with sweeping the wooden floors as the place began to close around 9:30 in the evening. At the end of that first day in my fledgling career as one of Bob May's novitiates, I had earned a whopping $3…in cash.

By the time I entered high school, I moved up the ranks and became captain of the delivery crew. Inkspot was my worthy associate, and we would deliver groceries to customers all over town. You ring, and the two of us would definitely bring. Throughout the day, people would call in their list of grocery needs, and we would scurry through the store aisles collecting the desired goods.

Probably named for that infamous singing group of the 1940's, Inkspot was my cohort in our work, but our world would not let us be more than that because I was a white boy and he wasn't. History and religion and politics seemed to demand the order of things, including my relationship with my "brother from another mother". The only place we could have lunch was the Canton Sandwich Shop which was a horseshoe-shaped bar with a curtain to divide the customers by color. If we sat next to the curtain, we could talk. In spite of such nonsense, we encouraged each other's competitive work ethic by sharing our early commercial adventures in Bob May's WWII surplus jeep.

While our black and white worlds were segregated, we knew in our bones that we were of the same ilk and had each other's backs if push ever came to shove — as it most certainly would when I discovered how inadvertently Jim Crow's "separate but equal" principle created awful injustices for our "minority", who happened to be seventy-percent of our citizens unable to vote simply because of the color of their skin. Ink and I seldom talked about Brown vs. The Board of Education nor "critical race theories" that have put local boards of education in political quagmires as a way of erasing all of the progress made over several generations.

In addition to delivering groceries, Inkspot and I would be sent out at the end of the month to "collect" from customers who had not come to the store to settle their bills. In most instances, these were the people who lived "across the tracks" on much less income than most citizens. We would listen to their particular plights for the month and come to some sort of understanding as to when they would meet their obligation. There was a special little old lady for whom we would chip in from our meager pay to help her make her ends meet without ever letting Bob May know about it. She eventually repaid us, but the tie that bound us was priceless.

5/23/2021

# Tomb of the Unknown Children

Something dastardly caught my eye and broke my heart this week. A small article of news claiming that 68 children were killed in the Holy Land in the eleven days of fighting between the two ancient foes. As we observe our Memorial Day weekend in which we honor the memory of our soldiers killed in combat, why can't we also honor the memory of all the children who were innocent victims of all wars. Maybe establish international monuments, like the Tomb of the Unknown Children.

We might even consider honoring all those killed in all the wars ever by figuring out the source and a way to end them. A war on wars perhaps. Maybe a poet can shed some light here. Fifty years ago South African Kendrew Lascelles composed *The Box*, which aired on the Smothers Brothers Show in summer of 1971, and later recited by John Denver on his *Poems, Prayers, and Promises* album. Let me encourage us to read this poem out loud and listen to it as if it were both a prayer and a promise to all the children of the world.

*Once upon a time, in the land of Hush-A-Bye,*

*Around about the wondrous days of yore,*

*They came across a kind of box*

*Bound up with chains and locked with locks*

*And labeled "Kindly do not touch; it's war."*

*A decree was issued round about, and all with a flourish and a shout*

*And a gaily colored mascot tripping lightly on before.*

*Don't fiddle with this deadly box, Or break the chains, or pick the locks.*

*And please don't ever play about with war.*

*The children understood. Children happen to be good*

*And they were just as good around the time of yore.*

*They didn't try to pick the locks Or break into that deadly box.*

*They never tried to play about with war.*

*Mommies didn't either; sisters, aunts, grannies neither*

*'Cause they were quiet, and sweet, and pretty*

*In those wondrous days of yore.*

*Well, very much the same as now,*

*And not the ones to blame somehow*

*For opening up that deadly box of war.*

*But someone did. Someone battered in the lid*

*And spilled the insides out across the floor.*

*A kind of bouncy, bumpy ball made up of guns and flags*

*And all the tears, and horror, and death that comes with war.*

*It bounced right out and went bashing all about,*

*Bumping into everything in store. And what was sad and most unfair*

Was that it didn't really seem to care

Much who it bumped, or why, or what, or for.

It bumped the children mainly. And I'll tell you this quite plainly,

It bumps them every day and more, and more,

And leaves them dead, and burned, and dying

Thousands of them sick and crying.

'Cause when it bumps, it's really very sore.

Now there's a way to stop the ball. It isn't difficult at all.

All it takes is wisdom, and I'm absolutely sure

That we can get it back into the box, And bind the chains, and lock the locks.

But no one seems to want to save the children anymore.

Well, that's the way it all appears, 'cause it's been bouncing round

for years and years

In spite of all the wisdom wizzed since those wondrous days of yore

And the time they came across the box,

Bound up with chains and locked with locks,

And labeled "Kindly do not touch; it's war."

5/30/2021

# How Critical Is Your Racial Theory?

Our local school board is fighting tooth and nail over an issue that most of us thought was gone with the wind. However, some of the throw backs among us believe that they should take some sort of imaginary last stand against godless communism threatening our wonderful white way of life. When you dissect this weird phenomenon, it's nothing but a head trip to avoid what the heart knows as a "little white lie" to a bigger truth about the mistreatment of African Americans since they arrived on these shores in the chains of chattel slavery to bolster plantation capitalism with free labor.

This mess going on right now started with the former President's executive order in September of 2020 prohibiting any federal contracts being awarded to any organization that promotes, among other notions, "critical racial theory" [CRT] which came out of academia in the 1970's. According to the American Bar Association, "CRT recognizes that racism is not a bygone relic of the past. Instead, it acknowledges that the legacy of slavery, segregation, and the imposition of second-class citizenship on Black Americans and other people of color continue to permeate the social fabric of this nation." Who can argue with that?

Way back in 1949, the hit musical *South Pacific* received scrutiny for its commentary regarding relationships between different races and ethnic groups. In particular, "You've Got to Be Carefully Taught" was subject to widespread criticism, judged by some to be too controversial or downright inappropriate for the musical stage. Sung by the character Lieutenant Cable, the song is preceded by a line saying racism is "not born in you! It happens after you're born..."

When you hear what is being sung, you can understand how a critical racial theory is already at work during and following World War II: *You've got to be taught to hate and fear/ You've got to be taught from year to year/ It's got to be drummed into your dear little ear/ You've got to be carefully taught.* The second verse builds on the racial theory: *You've got to be taught to be afraid/ Of people whose eyes are oddly made/ And people whose skin is a different shade...* The third and final verse drives it all home with a vengeance: *You've got to be taught before it's too late/ Before you are six or seven or eight/ To hate all the people your relatives hate/ You've got to be carefully taught.* Maybe this could become the theme song for our local school board; it might be more fitting than that "sweet land of liberty" song.

Funny how some history was seldom mentioned when I was being carefully taught "to hate all the people my relatives hate". No one explained how we ran off the first real Americans who were peacefully [though inconveniently] living on "our" land. We let them share Thanksgiving with us! Slave life on the plantations was regarded by our history and blessed by our religion as some kind of God-given privilege. Some of our shameful history just got lost. Whoever heard of the Tulsa race riots of 1921? That unholy siege on our Capitol on January 6 by white supremacist with rebel flags...never happened.

We've been grinding this axe for so long that it's become quite dull and meaningless. Maybe we should "bury the hatchet" like the first real Americans used to do. When two tribes decided to settle their differences and live in harmony, the chief of each tribe buried a war hatchet in the ground to signify their agreement. Wouldn't that be a lesson for us all?

6/6/2021

# Around the World in Sixty Minutes

Before television and internet, someone had to bear the burden of delivering the news hot off the press to folk in my little town. Paper boys would gather with their big-basket bicycles early every morning at the bus station to receive their route bundles. We would sit on the curbs and roll each edition with a rubber band or fold them into a flat square which would sail better when thrown from bike to porch. I hand tossed the "Clarion Ledger" each and every morning, come rain or shine, and finished in just about an hour.

 At the time I didn't appreciate the cultural capital on the receiving end of my labors and how these assorted varieties of human beings formed my worldview. For example, the Powell's house was your basic small-town mansion, and I was expected to drive silently through the porte-cochère, hand the paper to the butler each morning, and receive a dime tip from his white-gloved hand for the extra effort. Another favorite was Rabbi Max Lewinthal, who lived on the second floor of the old Grady Hotel on Fulton Street. He always went by "Rabbi" and often he invited me into his rather humble abode at six-thirty in the morning for some kind of kosher pastry and a bit of Yiddish wisdom.

My little town was quite cosmopolitan when it came to countries and religions of origin, and my job was to connect these people to the larger world by throwing the local and international news on their porches every morning. Most of the merchants were either Jewish or Lebanese who, like my own grandparents [with roots in Ireland and Scotland] in the late 1800's and early 1900's, had used the railways to find their way to the middle of Mississippi on the Illinois Central connecting Chicago and New Orleans. At its peak, Canton was home to Roman Catholics, Protestants, and approximately 100 Jewish families, all of whom brought their European cultural heritage and combined it with the cultures of the South: the Wieners from Germany, along with the Lehmann brothers who operated the movie theaters; the Perlinskys from Poland; the Hesdorffers from France. Our nearest neighbors included the Kaplans and the Rosens who were from Odessa in the Ukraine.

The Iupes and Saabs were from Lebanon, as was Waddell Thomas who owned and operated the Mecca Cafe. In 1967, three years after defeating Sonny Liston, Mohammed Ali drops by the Mecca through the kitchen door, of course, to visit with his wife's uncle who was a cook. Seizing the moment, Waddell runs out to the table full of his buddies and bets them he can produce the boxing champion right there and then. He did, they lost their bets, and there's a sign on the back of a chair claiming "Mohammed Ali sat here." That was "breaking news!" before the term became quite commonplace.

This was the town where many nationalities formed the *E Pluribus Unum* that took root in my soul. Growing up among the rich and varied ethnicities of such folks made me a lucky paper boy who appreciated all those dear hearts and gentle hometown people who taught me just how small the world was after all.

My luck, however, would run out on me at the end of the daily route. The major downside of this noble profession was the location of the paper drop off at the bus station where two pinball machines tenaciously tempted me to spend some of my hard-earned profit each week.

6/13/2021

# Be Kind to God Week

Once a year the little Methodist college I attended used to have what was called "Religious Emphasis Week", which some of us more cynical students referred to as "be kind to God week". With some reluctance, we went to chapel religiously for a whole week. I'm not sure how much God may have appreciated our perfect attendance.

Seems like there's a month or a day for everything under the sun. April brought us Earth Day and Arbor Day. Memorial Day and Labor Day are called the "bookends of the summer". Just this week Congress officially made Juneteenth a national holiday. Having already celebrated Mothers Day back in May, today happens to be the day to pay homage to all the dads, as if we should be nice to our parents at least annually if not perennially as the fifth commandment so nobly suggests.

Which brings us to the subject of gender and our current critical gender theory [CGT] with regard to God in particular. When I was being carefully taught about how I should believe, God was always referred to in masculine terms. The proper pronoun was always "He" or "Him" or "His" with a capital "h" to differentiate Him from mortal men. All of this stuff started coming unglued for me during one of my several mid-life crises and affected my role as minister for years to come.

The essence of this struggle with spiritual and gender undertones is summarized by Billy Bigelow's soliloquy in the great musical *Carousel*. After singing about how he would be a proud father to a his very own son Bill, he insists… "I will see that he's named after me…", he pauses and thinks out loud…"Wait a minute! Could it be? What the hell! What if he is a girl?...You can have fun with a son, but you gotta be a father to a girl."

When it finally dawned on me that all the stories of our faith were mostly written by a bunch of single guys, no wonder their god was pictured as not only an old white man with a beard, but as "Our Father, who art in heaven..." So, like Billy Bigelow, I began to wonder what if He is a She? For better or worse, I began to consider the ultimate option: does it really matter, one way or the other? Even though this flew in the face of everything I had been taught, it enabled me to perceive God quite freely and to finally be kind to God without perfect attendance.

Because I really liked my job as a minister, I did not flaunt my discovery of God's gender issues. However, I encountered several sticky points in dealing with the grammar of faith. Throughout scripture and creeds and hymns, God is always referred to as he, him and his. And a father figure. Over time, I figured out how to maneuver through those language minefields and began using inclusive language almost imperceptibly by changing all those pronouns to just God.

 Once you work through this, you become accustomed to the God who is not limited by genders or ethnicities. You are more at home with Martin Buber's "I and Thou". When you are free from trying to force God into all the images that have been created by humankind over the centuries, especially through the critical gender theory, your relationship with the Divine eases into an instinctive one that becomes second nature.

Like being in sync with Mother Nature herself, who today is pulling off another summer solstice without so much as a by your leave.

6/20/2021

# Without Malice for Absence

There's a wonderful country and western song entitled "How Can I Miss You If You Won't Go Away?" The sentiments expressed in that one are similar to Jimmy Buffet's "If the Phone Doesn't Ring, It's Me." These are musical ways of negatively expressing that marvelous maxim about absence making the heart grow fonder. Over the past year or so, absence has become quite commonplace.

During the depths of Covid time, I remember how much I missed seeing the people who would otherwise gather every Sunday in the sanctuary for worship if the medical establishment and the responsible government agencies had not brought down the curtain on such public gatherings. While congregations are once again congregating, I was reminded of a particular and sinful nuance, and I must admit to some guilt for not feeling guilty about missing church for at least two months [60+] of Sundays.

Way back in pre-pandemic days some of us might not have remembered the last time we went to worship or church school. When you showed up on any given Sunday, you might get a "where-in-the-world-have-you-been?' look from the minister or a friend might make some snide comment about renting your pew to someone else. The excuses for absence were probably valid ones: trips to the beach or to grandmas; the golf tournament; unexpected company; a day to be with the family; too cold, too hot, too wet, too tired. And the summertime was that season of the year when these occasions for no-show seem to multiply. Whatever the reasons or the seasons and no matter the length of absences, church folk felt a little guilty for being AWOL. It was a good guilt, but guilt to be exploited, nonetheless.

Further back in the good ol' days, the public library used to declare an amnesty on all overdue books to allow delinquents to return their goods without fear of fine or public humiliation. Others published "shame sheets" of the names of those who had books which should have been returned over a year ago. The book-keepers were scared to go in the library for fear of seeing their mug shots plastered on the bulletin boards. For many a reason, proper excuses can be made by the defendants. But, when all was said and done, they were guilty as charged and felt that slight sense of shame.

When I used to serve as a pastor under normal conditions, I felt we ought to have one or two "Amnesty Sundays" in the year, when absentee members could come back to the fold and not feel nervous or bothered about the consequences of their delinquencies. A day when they would have the sworn word of the minister that he or she would not call them by name, ask them to stand up and demand that they give a strict accounting of their whereabouts these past Sundays. And all the "faithful" members [who, of course, have perfect attendance records!] would not make abusive nor snide remarks or even think evil of their vagrant ways or indulgent Sabbaths.

Absence does make our hearts grow fonder while offering us a chance to welcome home all our sisters and brothers of the faith who have been "doing time" in their own far countries and are ready to head toward the house of the Lord. Rather than wondering about how much we missed them while they were away, let's open our arms and minds and hearts to welcome them home in the best tradition of that term. Sure beats sending them away on some absentee purgatory or an endless guilt trip to nowhere.

6/27/2021

# No More Communion for You!

All of this hullabaloo about withholding communion from the President until he yields to the pressure of Catholic bishops on the abortion issue reminds me of Seinfeld's Soup Nazi. Throw in Galileo's house arrest for daring to question the authority of the church's five-thousand-year-old flat earth or Martin Luther's heresy trials for questioning indulgences, and you have the makings for the most imperfect tempest in a teapot. And don't forget how the church and the empire started a mutual back-scratching thing during Constantine's time or when Henry VIII needed a handy divorce so he became the head knocker of his own church *extra cathedra*.

The current controversy over denying Communion to the President has its roots in this sordid history of the Church. The Roman Catholics used the power of exclusion from the sacraments as a way of forcing the adherents to walk the line. Protestants also used the same tacky tactics to keep their members pure from ungodly errors. Even Presbyterians were not above the fray when they used "communion tokens" suggested by John Calvin in 1560 for those who had kept to the straight and narrow to earn a ticket to the communion table and — by innuendo — to heaven itself.

The modern manifestations of this holy mess emerged from the 1973 Roe v. Wade decision of the Supreme Court which finally allowed women the right to choose to end a pregnancy. The issue became a political hot potato as well as dividing many communities of faith. Within a short time Roman Catholics and Christian evangelicals became strange bedfellows [to use an uncanny metaphor] and a power block of voters courted by the right wingers.

While the Constitution allowed these expressions of concern, the same Constitution said "Congress shall make no law respecting an establishment of religion, or prohibiting the free exercise thereof." Thus the abortion issue became the most controversial wedge issue dividing Christians in the United States leading to what may be called a critical communion theory [CCT].

Why in God's name didn't Moses, David, Bathsheba, Isaiah, Matthew, Paul, the Virgin Mary or even Jesus himself ever mention abortion as some kind of official sin in order to make it a religious reality? If the Bible doesn't say it, why do some fundamentalists believe it with such fervor? It has nothing to do with piety and everything to do with politics and the power to create a religious nation that's run just like Iran.

To the religiously righteous, unwanted pregnancy outside what used to be called "wedlock" was the result of participating in what many consider the most original sin of all. Pregnancy was equated with the punishment of such a crime…at least the woman's complicity in it. In Nathaniel Hawthorne's *Scarlet Letter*, Hester Prynne was forced to wear the big A as punishment to declare her sin of Adultery which would inadvertently lead to the birth of her daughter Pearl. Today that same letter could be used to declare Abortion a top-rated "cardinal" sin without a single biblical reference.

When I first started serving communion to the Presbyterian faithful, children were not allowed to partake because some older white men known as our Elders thought kids would not understand its mystery and meaning. Maybe the same can be said of some bishops these days who take it upon themselves to limit the amazing grace of God. To paraphrase Jesus… *unless you become like Pearl and other children, you can't enter the Kingdom and there'll be no more communion.*

7/4/2021

# A Prayer for Growing Older

I have always lived on a wing and a prayer without ever believing that prayer changes God's mind or much of anything else. The first prayer I can remember was the "blessing" at every meal: "Bless this food to our use and us to Thy service. Amen" Never could figure out such words that were repeated each and every day no matter the menu.

The scariest prayer I learned as a child was that bedtime ditty: "Now I lay me down to sleep; I pray the Lord my soul to keep. If I should die before I wake, I pray the Lord my soul to take." Made you think twice about falling too deeply into sleep.

By the time we reached fifth grade most of us could recite the Lord's Prayer by heart. I was never quite sure about who our father that was in heaven nor what the kingdom and the glory were forever and ever. The whole thing was a bit too full of fanciful figments of imagination to really have any traction. And you always had to worry about "debts" and "trespasses" and exactly who did and who didn't.

The best secular prayer I know was set to song in 1970 by Janis Joplin: *O lord won't you buy me a Mercedes Benz./ My friends all drive Porsches, I must make amends./ Worked hard all my lifetime, no help from my friends./ So oh lord won't you buy me a Mercedes Benz?* She then goes on to pray for a "color tv" and "a night on the town." Practical things!

Prayer was a required skill for my chosen profession, and I always had to be ready to bless any moment without a moment's notice. Such serendipity prayers usually came with more candor than those pastoral prayers that were expected during the Sunday morning worship service, many of which could be had for a dime a dozen in all sorts of liturgical books.

Seems like there's a prayer for everything under the sun… like stardust itself. I haphazardly "stumbled" over an anonymous prayer that seemed so fitting for my later years; perhaps, it will fit you as well.

*Lord, Thou knowest better than I know myself that I am growing older and will someday be old. Keep me from the fatal habit of thinking I must say something on every subject and on every occasion. Release me from the craving to straighten out everybody's affairs. Make me thoughtful but not moody; helpful but not bossy. With my vast store of wisdom, it seems a pity not to use it all but Thou knowest Lord, that I want a few friends at the end. Keep my mind free from the recital of endless details… give me wings to get to the point. Seal my lips on my aches and pains. They are increasing, and love of rehearsing them is becoming sweeter as the years go by. I dare not ask for patience to enjoy the tales of others, but help me to endure them with understanding. I dare not ask for improved memory but a growing humility and a lessening cocksureness when my memory seems to clash with the memories of others. Teach me the glorious lesson that occasionally I may be mistaken. Keep me reasonably sweet. I do not want to be a saint — some of them are so hard to live with. Give me the ability to see good things in unexpected places and talents in unexpected people. Give me the ability to tell them. Amen.*

9/12/2021

285

# The Summer of Our Discontent

Written in 1961, the title of John Steinbeck's final novel, The Winter of Our Discontent, was based on a term from Shakespeare's play about Richard III. The story mainly concerns Ethan Allen Hawley, a former member of Long Island's aristocratic class. Ethan's late father lost the family fortune, and thus Ethan works as a grocery store clerk which is exactly what I was doing in my freshman year in college to make ends meet while reading the Steinbeck novel each evening. The continuous calamities within the book's plot made my life seem more like Shangri-La and gave me a perspective on just how pernicious things can become.

When people needed a term to describe what seemed to be the worst of times, the phrase was adapted to the particular season of their discontent. In a recent column entitled "Here Comes the Autumn of Anxiety", economist Paul Krugman wrote, *In the heady days of spring, when the United States was vaccinating 3 million people a day, President Biden predicted a "summer of joy." But then the vaccination campaign stalled, and the Delta variant fueled a new wave of infections, hospitalizations, and deaths.* After good research on the reasons, Krugman concluded: *There's no mystery about why this has happened: It's political. The systematic refusal to get vaccinated, refusal to wear masks, etc., is very clearly tied to the unique way that common-sense public health measures have been caught up in the culture war.*

Just think about all the havoc that's been wreaked around here this past summer. Covid19 recreating itself into a longer world-wide pandemic. Hurricane Ida doing her dead level best to leave an awful path of damage. Our troops and allies pulling out of

Afghanistan after the longest war in our nation's history. The lone star state of Texas has banned abortions, created vigilantes with the responsibility to police the pregnancy policy for bounty money, granted everyone the right to tote a gun without a license, enabled poll watchers to intimidate people at the voting polls and restricted other voting rights creating a haven for havoc everywhere. And we must never forget those home-grown terrorists who attacked our nation's capital in an act designed to overthrow democracy, just like what happened 20 years ago on 9/11 by foreign terrorist.

All of these calamities created a domino effect that landed smack dab in the middle of this summer of discontent. Few of them can hold a candle to the quiet elephant in the atmosphere: global warming that spans all our seasons and takes our breath away as we watch nature ignite with forest fires and fill our streets with flood waters.

Twenty years ago, when this country was attacked on September 11, those hijacked planes certainly created a holy terror from which we continue to shake in our boots on or off the ground. And even now as we leave our longest war that was started to avenge that day, we are still wreaking its havoc. Those mysterious weapons of mass destruction that led to the illusion of another war have finally and tragically turned out to be just another mirage based on a lie. As we get ready to contend with another cold winter, may we be helped and haunted by those words from T.S. Elliot's epic poem, *The Hollow Men*: "This is the way the world ends... not with a bang but with a whimper."

9/19/2021

# The Contagious Catch of Curiosity

Magicians were few and far between during my sordid youth, but I'll never forget the magic spell they cast on me and the others in their audience. White rabbits were extracted from black hats. Some beautiful lady was sawn in half. A volunteer just disappeared right before our eyes. Slight of hands made card decks do wonders. It would take days to unscramble all that hocus pocus of the curious magician on our school stage.

Certain human attributes are both helpful and hurtful. Like a magnet, they seem to have two poles: one positive and the other negative. Or, perhaps these qualities are better captured in the Chinese philosophy which perceives all of life made up of opposites, which are called the yin and yang. While curiosity killed the proverbial cat, it has also led to life-saving discoveries like the long-awaited vaccine. Wisdom is achieved by balancing these opposing forces.

Curiosity is a clear example of one of those insatiable characteristics we bear in common as humans. We enter this existence with curiosity and spend our childhood and youth satisfying this appetite to know more about this universe home of ours. We have this innate feeling that something unknown is doing we don't know what, but we aim to find out.

Curiosity has been at the heart of scientific discoveries that have led to cures or geographic adventures that have founded new countries. And in the field of religion, this natural curiosity sends us all to discover something about the nature of a possible Creator, no matter what name we give. If we dare, we even become curious about ourselves.

Physicist and chemist Marie Curie warned that we should "Be less curious about people and more curious about ideas." When curiosity downgrades itself into prying nosiness or tacky meddling, that noble virtue of wonder has now turned itself toward plunder. We use curiosity as a survival tactic in the game of being one up on thy neighbor. Or maybe we play the less harmful game of simply being curious for the sake of knowing what's up. When we know that, then we can keep ourselves clean as a whistle — detached and disinterested and safe.

Lulu Miller, in her recent book, Why Fish Don't Exist, puts it like this: "The best way to ensure you don't miss them [the good things in store], these gifts, the trick that has helped me squint at the bleakness and see more clearly, is to admit, with every breath, that you have no idea of what you are looking at. To examine each object in the avalanche of Chaos with curiosity, with doubt."

Curiously, there is very little in the Good Book about the subject. At least on the lines. In between the lines, one discovers the same game at work. The yin and the yang of curiosity. Remember Lot's wife. Or Job's quest for figuring out God. Paul struggling to understand himself. On the Jericho road, the Scribe and the Pharisee were only curious about that victim. Somehow, in the life of Jesus, we see in the absence of the subject, the very presence of someone who has figured out the balance. He operates from the perspective that is more caring than curious. Like the Samaritan, he sees that victim's need more than he wonders about the cause of what will happen if he gets involved. He never stoops to snoop, but accepts people where they are, as they are. Like us, though, even

Jesus had his moments. He died with that ultimate curiosity: "My God, why...?" Wouldn't we really like to know.

9/26/2021

# How Well Is It with Your Soul?

Proper Presbyterian protocol demanded that I be brought up in the "nurture and admonition" of the church. In my case, they had to go heavy on the "admonition". One of the tools employed in my indoctrination was the Westminster Catechism, beginning with the Children's edition which asked "What else did God give Adam and Eve beside a body?" Answer: "God gave them souls that will never die." [Remember, they did not have belly buttons!] Question 19: "Have you a soul as well as a body? Answer: Yes, I have a soul that will never die."

As Answer 20 and the bumper sticker exclaim "The Bible says it; I believe it; that settles it." Whoa! Can't we just hold our horses here a minute and do a bit of soul searching? Out here on the outer orbits of my little personal existence, I'm having a hard time with stuff related to the after life. Will I finally get to meet friendly Casper? Will the words of Blood, Sweat and Tears "I know there ain't no heaven, but pray there ain't no hell" come to life at my death?

Before that comes to past, bear with me as I bare what proports to be my soul on this matter that seems to matter to some people. If we check out "soul" in the Merriam-Webster, we find ourselves on several pages at once: *1] the spiritual part of a person that is believed to give life to the body and in many religions is believed to live forever; 2] a person's deeply felt moral and emotional nature; 3] the ability of a person to feel kindness and sympathy for others, to appreciate beauty and art, etc.*

According to Andrea Lynn's internet article: *The term "soul food" didn't become common until the 1960s. With the rise of the civil rights and Black nationalist movements during the 1960s, many Black Americans sought to reclaim their part of the American cultural legacy. As terms like "soul brother," "soul sister," and "soul music" were being used, and people began to use the term "soul food" to describe the recipes that Black Americans had been cooking for generations.* As a native son of Mississippi, that soul power was all over me like white on rice.

Let's get to the juicy stuff before we run out of space here. When Ella Fitzgerald sings her semi-sultry song, you need to remember that Westminster Catechism, written in Edinburgh in 1648. King Charles was about to literally lose his head, and Cromwell's folk were stirring the Puritan pot of dissent. The framers were insistent on separating the soul from our nasty bodies. So how dare this lady of soul music sing such a song: *My heart is sad and lonely! /For you I sigh, for you dear only/ Why haven't you seen it?/ I'm all for you Body and Soul.*

That classic hymn "It Is Well with My Soul" points us to a flaw in this soul-searching endeavor. When you listen to the words, you can't help but be struck by a note of spiritual narcissism that finds its source in the quaint Catechism mentality that pushes us to just worry about our own souls and the devil take the hindmost. As I understand the very heart and soul of the Gospel, that until we are all soul brothers and soul sisters who see that all bodies and souls matter in God's scheme for the greater good, we're just embellishing ghost stories from seventeenth century England while whistling Dixie.

10/3/2021

# Ain't It Awful!

Lately, I've been playing the "ain't it awful" card on some of our blogs to show us just how far we are up that proverbial creek without a paddle to our name. The term could easily be used for many of the newsworthy events of the day, especially during this Covid19 pandemic and all the political quagmires and shenanigans that consume the news, like the insurrection of January 6 or Texas outlawing abortions with wild west tactics where bounty hunters can wear their guns to town to nab those suspicious would-be mothers.

On a more personal level, most of us experience so many dilemmas throughout our lives and especially all that we've been through for the past couple of years. It has its locus somewhere between a rock and a hard place, and there's usually no place to put your fulcrum to lift yourself out of the morass. Conflicts with the spouse or children or parents that seem irresolvable. Financial crunches or reversals. Depression and despair. Even Facebook using us to stoke anger and hate. Ain't it awful!

Enter the panhandlers and fix-it philosophers with all sorts of wares for the people in such predicaments. One says: "Such difficulty is merely a state of mind. So if you'll just work on your mind, you can always win in such matters. Harness your wagon to the power of positive thinking, and you'll obliterate anything that prevents you from fulfilling your wonderful self." Another peddles consumerism: "Fill it up to the brim with all these goodies and gadgets and go for it all. Shop 'til you drop. As the old poet put it 'getting and spending we lay waste our powers...'" Even evangelists claim a desirable form of "good news": "Let God be your co-pilot of convenience. You won't need to steer anymore. Nor think. Nor feel. Just glide the rest of the way to glory land. The world might be in a hell of a mess, but don't fret. No problem."

Perhaps the most glaring problem in the human predicament is our perpetual blindness that prohibits our seeing that things could actually be worse than they are. The old half-empty and/or half-full glass thing. The calming ability to look around us and see how good life is in spite of all things to the contrary. Once we see that light in our darkness, we can face so many of the awful predicaments that come our way.

 I vividly remember seeing such a small and subtle point of light many years ago. We had arrived in one of those villages in Wales whose name was beyond pronouncing, when a sudden rain shower just showed up out of nowhere. Our group of "Crawford Travelers" was caught unaware in the middle of some quaint shops and seemed to be outdone with this pesky change in the weather. During their whining and complaining, I happen to overhear some little old nearby Welsh woman exclaim to her friend, *"Could be worse; could be lashing!"*

Such a subtle yet extraordinary exclamation was like stumbling over a big pile of stardust. For the rest of that particular trip and for all the trips that would follow, that little phrase from that tiny Welsh lady became a mantra and a watchword to reorient our internal gyroscopes toward seeing the inherent good in just about all we would encounter on our lives' journeys.

10/10/2021

# Who Was That Unmasked Man?

Most of us have grown accustomed to utilizing masks to prevent the spread of this crazy and careless Covid19 virus. We have seen the science and understand that vaccines and masking really do the job in bringing down those morbid statistics. And if more of us would live by these gracious truths, we could save more of us from death.

But the proverbial fly has landed in this ointment of cure. The devil in disguise this time is the politics of misinformation. I try to be considerate of others and wear my mask in most public buildings like the post office or grocery store, and I appreciate those who make an effort to do the same for the greater good of the whole community. This week, however, there was a fellow in the frozen food aisle without a mask, and he was wearing a loaded revolver holstered under his arm. Could have been worse; he could have been smoking and drinking posing even more lethal threats to our safety because of his own dear God-given freedoms.

Masks are also associated with the art of masquerading. The New Webster's Dictionary & Thesaurus of the English Language define "masquerading" as "to wear a disguise, to put on a false outward show." Thus, the familiar "masquerade ball" is an event where the participants all wear masks, such as became a popular scene in the infamous musical, "Phantom of the Opera." For practical meaning, it alludes to "a false show for pretense or concealment of the truth". While masquerading might be fun recreationally, it becomes a serious problem when it enters the political or spiritual realms. The Bible describes those who spiritually masquerade.

The Apostle Paul had his problems with those want-to-be-Christian Greeks in Corinth. Lots of wolves around there wearing all sorts of masks and pulling lots of sheep wool over your eyes. So in chapter eleven of Two Corinthians, Paul warns them: *for such people are false apostles, deceitful workers, masquerading as apostles of Christ. 14 And no wonder, for Satan himself masquerades as an angel of light.*

Flip Wilson was one of the great television comedians from the 1970's, and the character of Geraldine Jones still lingers with one of her favorite phrases: "the Devil made me do it." I found that a very useful excuse on several occasions. The Apostle Paul promptly brings down the curtain on such an act by letting us know that even Satan masquerades as an angel. As Martin Luther puts it in that great hymn of his: *And though this world, with devils filled, should threaten to undo us, we will not fear, for God has willed God's truth to triumph through us. The prince of darkness grim, we tremble not for him; his rage we can endure, for lo! his doom is sure; one little word shall fell him.*

Inherent in all of this is the idea of a drama between good and evil, truth and lies. As the Bard reminds us: *All the world's a stage,/ And all the men and women merely players;/ They have their exits and their entrances...* He also exclaims through Polonius in Hamlet: *This above all: to thine own self be true, And it must follow, as the night the day,/ Thou canst not then be false to any man.* If only such wisdom would undergird our reality in these days, and if the truth be known, we would once again discover a balm in

Gilead that would make the wounded whole and cure the soul of our sick nation.

10/17/2021

# Civilizing Citizens with Couth & Culture

We have had immigration issues since heaven knows when, but it began when those white European invaders started taking over native American lands in order to bring in slaves from Africa to see if capitalism would work with free labor. The art of the treaty was used to bring about this change, and military power was used to ratify everything.

The Doak's Stand Treaty was invented in my part of Mississippi in 1820 and served as good example of how great a deal this was for the Choctaw tribes whose land was about to be had for plantations. They were "free" to move to Arkansas with the rest of their kind if they would sell their tract of land to white settlers and use the profit to pay for that trip along the trail of tears. For those who wanted to stay put the following article was part of the Treaty: *The boundaries hereby established between the Choctaw Indians and the United States, on this side of the Mississippi river, shall remain without alteration until the period at which said nation shall become so civilized and enlightened as to be made citizens of the United States, and Congress shall lay of a limited parcel of land for the benefit of each family or individual in the nation. ...*

Becoming "civilized and enlightened" involved giving up more than just the land. They had to change their ways of dressing; their religion would necessarily become Christian; and they had to think like the white folk who had stolen their birthrights in the name of some manifest destiny that formed this nation's core value. None of this was to be mentioned in history for the sake of critical racial theories.

Many moons ago, one of our kids came home from middle school and let us know that the social studies teacher was skipping the chapter on Native Americans. His reason: all they do is whine. That's a pretty critical approach to racial differences, in theory and in practice.

Here's an enlightening quote from the Library of Congress: "It's often overlooked that self-government in America was practiced by Native Americans long before the formation of the United States government. And yet, Native Americans faced centuries of struggle before acquiring full U.S. citizenship and legal protection of their voting rights." Only "civilized and enlightened" Americans, those with couth and culture, enough education to read and write, and some wherewithal, deserve the right to vote!

This also applied to African Americans. In 1961, less than 7% of Mississippi Blacks were registered to vote. And of those few on the voter rolls, only a handful dared to actually cast a ballot. You must remember that the literacy test required a person seeking to register to vote to read a section of the state constitution and explain it to the white county clerk who processed voter registrations. When I went to register to vote during this time, I offered to help an older and obviously illiterate black couple read the state's constitution. The clerk told me to mind my own business, and that particular voting discrepancy has been my business ever since.

 History has a ferocious and finicky way of repeating and contradicting itself. Remember the great horned hoodlum [or ill-clad tourist] in Trump's militaristic minions who led the insurrection against

our nation on January 6? He and his political cronies favor even more voter suppression, pointing to a pitiful deficit in their own couth and culture. Maybe all he and his kind can do is whine.

10/24/2021

# Hawks Need to Prey

Remember the good old days when we used to wonder if our children could ever pray again in school? The bumper sticker campaign that had emerged every now and then was "Kids Need to Pray". The drivers of such vehicles fervently believed that the American God listed on our dollar bills as in whom we trust, was anxiously waiting for school prayers to earnestly begin each school day, along with the pledge of allegiance to the flag. We added "under God" to that pledge in 1954 to cover all bets.

When I was a kid in the 50's, I prayed a lot in school but for lesser reasons than one may be led to think. I discovered that the prayer for better grades did not really work. After one particular Halloween, I prayed that the "trick" we pulled would go undiscovered and never blamed on the actual culprits. That did not work out, either.

I loved the counter sticker to "Kids Need to Pray" that emerged on a few bumpers: "Hawks Need to Prey". This subtly stated a more practical truth and did not run counter to the United States Supreme Court ruling in 1963 that government mandated school prayer is unconstitutional under the Establishment Clause of the First Amendment. This might have been when some of us began "Thank You, Jesus" slogans which now seem to populate many front yards here in the South.

When I arrived in the old south as the young minister, this issue of prayer in public schools was in full bloom, and I was conned into many forms of praying that made me feel un-American at times. I recall being asked to pray over bunches of things like the county commissioner meetings or Friday night football games. I was always uneasy when some of my more evangelical counterparts ended such public prayers with hype and fervor "in the powerful name of Jesus who is our only way to salvation…" When the high school principal called to ask me to offer the football pre-game prayer on Friday night, I asked him to invite my friend the local rabbi or the catholic priest. The pregnant pause on the other end of the line spoke volumes.

I remember praying for a breath of fresh air in some restaurants that had ash trays on every table. Before 1964, smoking was a rampant way of life for many Americans, and the tobacco industry advertised heavily in the early days of television until the Surgeon General added his scientific findings on each pack. During the early 1960's, "Stop Smoking" started with an ad campaign that woke us all up to this other killer that ravaged primary smokers and second-hand smoke inhalers who needed to breathe. And we all know why George Floyd used his final minute to say, "I can't breathe!" for another tragic reason altogether.

Currently, bumpers bear the slogan "Kids Need to Breathe", counteracting mask mandates and the medical profession's wisdom that masks reduce the spread of Covid19. [In 50 years those adults might find it difficult to breathe after our nonchalance exhausts the air supply.] Funny, how we use the kids as political pawns in the games we play so that the kings and queens and their diagonally-moving praying bishops may reign forever on the chess board and in realms of the American way of life. Who cares if the kids get sick and die from pandemics or smoking or guns or lies or our many forms of phony faith masks? Maybe the only answer to our prayer is the silence at the other end of the line.

10/31/2021

# What's In Your Wallet?

Church signs have always intrigued me and helped me ponder the eternal question of who could think up that stuff? How about this one: "God recycles and all of us came from dust" [think *stardust*]. One of my favorite signs is "If God had a wallet, would your picture be in it?"

For what seems like forever, Capital One has been pushing their credit cards by asking "What's in your wallet?". Or maybe you get those very personal letters like I do: "Dear William Dudley Crawford, did you know that you already qualify for $10,000 credit? By simply completing the enclosed application and returning it, William Dudley Crawford, we will send you your new credit card and $10,000 instant credit."

How did they get my name? And how do they know enough about me to say I'm good for at least ten grand, even at their exorbitant interest rates? I already have that little piece of plastic with all those numbers and expiration date clearly embossed on its surface. And that wonderful chip and black strip that allows the cashier to zip the details of my purchase to some accounting Wizard of Oz who posts my debt on a giant screen which is constantly being scrutinized by the credit card gods who invented these gadgets to tempt us into an easy-come-easy-go mentality. I like that buy-to-fly card where the more you spend the more travel miles you earn!

Indebtedness aside, we all keep hearing about the expanding credit card debt in this country and world-wide. Some economists claim it's a necessary evil in a consumer-driven economy like ours. The revenue and jobs created by charge cards justify the over-indebtedness of so many people. And lawyers are benefiting with the significant increase in bankruptcy work.

For the sake of finishing what I started with this creditable conversation, let's convert the financial issues into a more theological paradigm — like our relationship with God Almighty. Churches talk about "saving" souls, and I've known preachers who take "credit" for saving so many in any given year. I've talked with lots of people who felt obliged to let me know how they had been "saved", and how they have been working ever since to earn credits with God in order to get into heaven.

Paul Scherer, great theologian and preacher at Union Theological Seminary in New York a generation ago, gave us a beautiful picture of this God we worship: "Love is a spendthrift, leaves its arithmetic at home and is always 'in the red'. And God is love."

The God of the gospels, as best I can make out, is more like a credit card entrepreneur who endows us with the gift of life. God takes stock in the creation and grants us more credit than we give ourselves at times or that we deserve. God's got our number, our net worth, and understands that we all have an expiration date. And this God is more concerned about how we spend this fortune of grace and mercy than about how nice we've been in order to save our own hides. This God seems more impressed by those lives that are spent rather than those who are saved.

11/7/2021

# Rekindling the Kindness of Kindergarten

How would you have liked operating a kindergarten for 28 students in your home in 1947? That's exactly what my grandmother, Mamaw, did in her modest three-bedroom home on Academy Street in Canton, Mississippi. She had served as the midwife for many of us and was an RN. A kind-hearted Yankee transplant from the Upper Peninsula of Michigan, she also served as the pianist for our Presbyterian Church. "Yours truly" is the blonde kid with the dumfounded look standing between Becky Southerland and Penny Estess near the middle of the back row.

If you were fortunate enough to have gone to kindergarten, you will certainly remember some of the important life lessons we learned as a bedrock for the other aspects of education that would demand our attention in the coming years. I don't remember taking a test or making a grade in kindergarten, but here are a few lessons we all learned from a list in a wonderful book by Unitarian minister Robert Fulghum:

1. *Share everything.*
2. *Play fair.*

3. *Don't hit people.*

4. *Put things back where you found them.*

5. *CLEAN UP YOUR OWN MESS.*

6. *Don't take things that aren't yours.*

7. *Say you're SORRY when you HURT somebody.*

8. *Wash your hands before you eat.*

9. *Flush.*

10. *Warm cookies and cold milk are good for you.*

11. *Live a balanced life – learn some and drink some and draw some and paint some and sing and dance and play and work everyday some.*

12. *Take a nap every afternoon.*

13. *When you go out into the world, watch out for traffic, hold hands, and stick together.*

I do remember number 12 because we each had our floor mats, and we did naps in two shifts because there were so many of us. Josephine would supervise the napping while Mamaw would be teaching the others in the back bedroom/classroom. We learned to mind our manners almost by osmosis, which is essentially doing all those things in that list above.

From kindergarten we went forth to matriculate, graduate, and earn degrees in higher education. But in kindergarten, we were given the principles of what counted and how to be kind. We had note pads from Coca-Cola with the golden rule imprinted on their flimsy covers: "Do Unto Others As You Would Have Others Do Unto You!"

As I watch all this meaningless falderal that goes on at boards of education meetings in our little county and throughout this country, I wonder if these people ever went to kindergarten to learn how to get along with others. Using public education as a weapon for political poppycock is just that, and it diminishes the worth of those wonderful teachers and students who just happen to be in range of their unilateral meanness. While illustrating a lack of manners they should have learned long ago, their misbehavior seems so disrespectful to those teachers like Mamaw and all the rest of them in my lifetime.

Looking back through the corridor of my own little scholastic history, that kindergarten picture continues to haunt me like some sacred memory that still gives me hope for what we can make of the time ahead of us. Or as the Unitarian minister Robert Fulghum put it in All I Really Need to Know I Learned in Kindergarten : "*I believe that imagination is stronger than knowledge. That myth is more potent than history. That dreams are more powerful than facts. That hope always triumphs over experience. That laughter is the only cure for grief. And I believe that love is stronger than death.*"

11/14/2021

# What's a Communist, Anyway?

Fresh out of seminary and into a small-town congregation, I decided to add altruism to Halloween. This was the late 1960's, and we gathered all the children to go together in small groups of masked missionaries armed with their little collection boxes in quest of alms for UNICEF [United Nations Children's Fund].

The one memory that stood out from that evening was the question a little child posed at the end of this worthy endeavor: "What's a communist?" When I asked why she wanted to know, she said that a certain household closed the door and told her that they would not contribute to anything that was "communist". While that might seem like a conundrum to some folk, that one word was a simple statement designed to confuse even a kid from the church who simply wanted to help hungry children.

After the bipartisan passage of the infrastructure bill this past week, Trump loyalists have demonized the bill as "Joe Biden's Communist takeover of America". There's that fearful word again. The scapegoat word during last year's election for the likes of others like us was "socialists". You start slinging words like that around everywhere, people get so scared they shut their doors and refuse to give credence to any other arguments even if the hungry children will be saved from starvation by your little coins in this Trick-or-Treat for UNICEF box.

When I was growing up in the middle of Mississippi, word was that anything north of Memphis was in communist country. When I headed to Richmond for seminary in 1964, folk in my home church warned me that many of the faculty members there were godless communists. I discovered that all of the professors there were as American as apple pie, and Richmond was just a hotbed of social rest. I remember attending a meeting of Southern Presbyterians where we were warned that if we ever re-united with those Northern Presbyterians, we were opening the doors to the communist who lived in Michigan. Since my grandmother had come from there, their warning seemed more like an idle tale full of sound and fury and signifying nothing in particular.

Through it all, my crap detector was worn out trying to nail down who and where all these communists were. Way back in 1950's, Senator McCarthy had a list of 205 names of "known communist" who were working for the State Department. He went after Hollywood with a vengeance by naming playwright Lillian Hellman as the worst of all. [read her Scoundrel Time] J. Edgar Hoover's war on the "Red Menace" named Eleanor Roosevelt and Martin Luther King, Jr. as prime suspects. The northern college students who came to my hometown to encourage our segregated citizens to register to vote were called "outside communist agitators".

The little girl's innocent question that Halloween night still haunts me, but I have realized that "communist" is merely a term we use to vilify those "other people" who are not like us. And we've been "othering" each other all our lives as we try to decide just who in the hell we are for heaven's sake. At least we are not one of **them**!

It's the gospel truth, and Jesus tried his best to keep us from "othering" people who were not like us. Because he sided with outsiders and said we should become like that inquisitive child, the righteous folks, along with the empire, suspected him of being a godless communist. According to that ancient creed, "he was crucified, dead and buried" before going to hell with all those "others".

11/21/2021

# Thanksgiving in Troublesome Times

Picture the first Thanksgiving in that poetic pose we've always imagined with freshly arrived Pilgrims and the original American patriots sitting around a bountiful table with turkey, dressing and all the trimmings. I wonder if they burst into a round of "This land is your land; this land is my land" or did the natives find it hard to imagine who these pale faces were and what language they were speaking. Did they wonder about what the lack of immigration laws would do to their peaceful lives so in tune with the land that belonged to all of the people.

Never in their wildest imaginations did those first Americans think that they just might get swindled out of their own country and end up in Oklahoma. Or that all those treaties they signed would not be worth the paper on which they were printed. The artist rendition shows a subdued scene of the originals and their peace pipe and a white guy with his long gun over his shoulder just to the left of center in the upper group looking for any sort of trouble that might erupt so that he could shoot in self-defense, like they do in Wisconsin and get away with murder. [*The First Thanksgiving* by Jean Leon Gerome Ferris, 1930]

We all know that our culture is a far cry from the one into which the original pilgrims wandered, and our prayers can't hold a candle to theirs. And yet I believe that in spite of all the affluence and arrogance around us, there is inside each and every immigrant on the face of this good earth a hunger for the stuff that money cannot buy and this realization that we do not live by bread or cranberry sauce or fossil fuels alone. In spite of appearances to the contrary, we live in an empty world that will call upon us all to pick up that pilgrim spirit in order to bring peace and hope in a world going mad between those who have too much and those who have hardly anything.

So come ye thankful people come, raise the song of harvest home, but also come admitting that the nation that's counting its blessings is a country of dire differences: between the filthy rich and the dirt poor; the well-fed and the malnourished; the well-healed and the ones without medical care at all. Deeply held convictions of white supremacy seem to have wandered back into the broad daylight to disrupt everything from school board meetings to democracy itself. Throw in to all of this the climate crises that will bring it all to an end before we know it, you'd have to agree that these are indeed troublesome times.

Just weeks before she died, Anne Frank, that sixteen year old victim of the most heinous hate in recent history, says so succinctly what we all need to hear: *I see the world gradually being turned into a wilderness, I hear the ever approaching thunder, which will destroy us too, I can feel the sufferings of millions and yet, if I look up into the heavens, I think it will all come right, that this cruelty too will end, and that peace and tranquility will return again. In the meantime, I must uphold my ideals…*

11/28/2021

# If We Only Had One Religion

Just last month, Michael Flynn, the former U.S. Security Advisor who was just subpoenaed by a House select committee investigating the January 6 insurrection at the Capitol, told a crowd at Cornerstone Church in San Antonio, "If we are going to have one nation under God, which we must, we have to have one religion. One nation under God, and one religion under God." He was definitely "preaching to the choir" and was graciously welcomed by every hardcore evangelical in earshot. If he fails to be elected the next president, Mr. Flynn would be the first to apply for the equivalent of the ayatollah that tells the Iranian politicians how to apply religious dogma to their country's laws.

Empires and rulers since Constantine have made weird bedfellows with religions in their historical contexts, especially Christianity. But this new democracy of ours was to be different, and no one faith would be the religion for all of us. Mark Twain said it so well: (*Our forefathers fled their homeland and came to America) to enjoy their religion and, at the same time, prevent other folks from enjoying theirs.* Twain also said, *Man...is the only animal that has the True Religion–several of them.*

For the sake of a good argument, let's say that the Christian religion becomes top dog in this country founded on the principle of that there just won't be a dominant religion. The next question would then be which Christian faith would be on top of such a totem pole? Southern Baptists WASP's or AME Zionists? Roman Catholics already have a national prefix. Presbyterians are nothing more than Methodist with a drinking problem who can't afford to be an Episcopalian.

Adolf Hitler's Nazi party was able to persuade the Church in Germany to turn the other cheek and close their eyes as he executed the final solution on the Jewish race and religion. The American South used the Church to cajole the white folk into believing they were God's chosen race to perpetuate slavery as established by their bibles. When the consequential holy wars erupted, the Germans and the southerners claimed that "their" god was on their sides. The words on the Nazi belt buckle *Gott Mits Uns* (God is With Us) competed with our "*In God We Trust*".

You might recall Jerry Falwell's Moral Majority, which he launched in 1979 to lobby for "pro-traditional family values." He used to say, "Get saved, get baptized, and get registered to vote," almost putting them on the same level of importance. One of Falwell's "family values" was to keep women in their place at home by lumping issues like the Equal Rights Amendment, the feminist movement, birth control, and abortion together in order to make them a giant wedge political issue. If you dig deeper, the ultimate goal was to protect segregated schools without showing your hand. The Moral Majority — which was neither — created a holy mess with their one true religion.

For the sake of another argument, let's say Michael Flynn and his political cronies were subpoenaed and put on trial before the American Inquisition for **being** Christians. Would there be enough evidence to convict them? And if you are one of those who just loves quoting scripture at your enemy, what will you do with the closing verses of Matthew 25 where nations themselves will be judged by how they treated the hungry and the thirsty and the sick and the poor and the strangers in their land rather than their pro-traditional family values or their brand name like the Cornerstone Church in Texas.

12/5/2021

# Chasing Rainbows & Fighting Windmills

While stumbling down many stardust paths since heaven knows when, several life-changing quests have led me up many mountains and down several rabbit holes. Musical movies planted seeds in my psyche and soul many miles back, and I've never been able to shake their impacts on how I see the world. *The Wizard of Oz* put me on the yellow brick road for a spell, where Dorothy and I were "always chasing rainbows, watching clouds drifting by... waiting to find a bluebird in vain..." But thanks to our dear special needs friends, we kept going until we found our Emerald City together.

Even after encountering the Wicked Witch of the West, we skipped and sang together that we "were off to see the Wizard, the wonderful Wizard of Oz." The Lion in desperate need of courage; the Tinman in need a heart; and the Scarecrow lacking a brain. Or so they all thought. As the song by America put it: "Oz never did give nothing to the Tin Man that he didn't already have..."

Somewhere along the trail, I ran full force into Don Quixote, *The Man of la Mancha*, and his invaluable sidekick, Sancho. Their quest was to "Dream the impossible dream; to fight the unbeatable foe; to bear with unbearable sorrow; to run where the brave dare not go." Even "to march into hell for a heavenly cause." The landscape for this quest was the Iberian Peninsula which happen to be full of windmills that Quixote mistook for dreaded giants. "Look your worship", said Sancho; "What we see there are not giants but windmills, and what seem to be their arms are sails that turned by the wind make the millstone go."

The other haunting song from a musical movie that set me thinking in circles was nestled in the score by Michelle Legrand for *The Thomas Crown Affair* in 1968: *Round, like a circle in a spiral, like a wheel within a wheel, / Never ending or beginning on an ever-spinning reel,/Like a snowball down a mountain or a carnival balloon, / Like a carousel that's turning, running rings around the moon,/ Like a clock whose hands are sweeping past the minutes of its face,/ And the world is like an apple whirling silently in space,/ Like the circles that you find in the windmills of your mind!*

 While we are all stumbling over our stardust, our heads and hearts are always searching for rainbows and bluebirds. Like Don Quixote, our better angels are always looking for ways to make this a more just and beautiful world for all of us. To see life not just as it is but as it ought to be. As the curtain gets ready to end the drama, Quixote explains his magical vision behind his quest: *And the world will be better for this: That one man, scorned and covered with scars, Still strove, with his last ounce of courage, To reach ... the unreachable star ...*

With these final thoughts of having shared our Sunday mornings together, this edition of **Stumbling Over Stardust** brings down the final curtain on our adventure. Last one out, please turn off the lights! Thank each and every one of you for your diligent readership that kept this writer on his best behavior while still chasing rainbows and fighting windmills in his quest to find the wisdom of age itself. From now on, "all the world's a stage, and all the men and women merely players; they have their exits...", and that's my cue!

12/12/2021

# After Words
## Introducing the Back Cover

Mark Twain once reminded us that "Travel is fatal to prejudice, bigotry, and narrow-mindedness, and many of our people need it sorely on these accounts. Broad, wholesome, charitable views of people and things cannot be acquired by vegetating in one little corner of the earth all one's lifetime." His take on this human predicament happened to me over and over in those "faraway places with strange sounding names". My candid camera and I were fascinated by the lovely faces of all those people passing by in such a small and wonderful world after all. On the back of this book are a few of my photogenic cousins from all over this precious planet who only ask that we take the time to just look at each other and notice the family resemblances. This collage is the only snapshot I've ever taken of the God in whose image we all happen to be created.

While beauty may seem to be in the eye of the beholder, the beholder might just become the object of the art itself. When you cast your gaze upon these faces of these world-wide compatriots, let them gaze on your smiling countenance as if you just might both be beholders of a miracle itself.